Intimacy with Jesus

Verse by Verse
From the Song of Songs

Madame Guyon

Translated by James W. Metcalf, M.D.

I dedicate the republishing of this wonderful piece of literature to my beautiful godmother – *Pascale Gousseland.*

Though physical distance has kept us from seeing each other often, I thank God that she is in my life. She is an example of true kindness and steadfast patience. May the Lord bless her richly in the years to come.

Love you my Pascale!

CONTENTS

Preface   #1

Chapter 1   #3

Chapter 2   #27

Chapter 3   #43

Chapter 4   #55

Chapter 5   #69

Chapter 6   #85

Chapter 7   #101

Chapter 8   #111

PREFACE

I have never heard anyone expound on the Song of Songs with such deepness and understanding as Madame Guyon. This book is truly a gift to the body of Christ. Each verse is so carefully unwrapped, revealing the overwhelming love of God to us – *His beloved.*

Digest the contents of this book with patience and reflection. Each chapter is designed to be built upon. It truly is a story of our soul entering deeper and deeper into God, until there is only Him left.

Be blessed as you read this book my friend, and may it further your relationship with our glorious bridegroom – Jesus Christ.

William Crockett
President of GodSounds, Inc.

Madame Guyon

CHAPTER 1

THIS kiss, which the soul desires of its God, is essential union, or a real, permanent and lasting possession of its divine object. It is the spiritual marriage.

That this may be understood, it is necessary to explain the difference between a union of the powers and essential union. Either of them may be transitory, and for a few moments only, or permanent and lasting.

The union of the powers is that by which God unites the soul to Himself, but very superficially; it is more properly a contact than a union. It is nevertheless united to the personal Trinity according to the different effects peculiar to each member of it; but always as if to distinct persons, and by an intermediate operation. This operation serves both as a means and an end, the soul resting in the union

3

thus experienced, without supposing that there is anything beyond.

This union is accomplished in order, in all the powers of the soul, and is sometimes perceived in one or two of them according to the designs of God, and at others in all three together. This constitutes the application of the soul to the Holy Trinity as to distinct persons.

When the union is in the understanding alone, it is a union of pure intellect, and is attributed to the Word as a distinct person. When the union is in the memory, which is effected by an absorption of the soul into God, and a profound forgetfulness of the creature, it is attributed to the Father, as a distinct person. And when it takes place in the will alone, by a loving joy without sight or knowledge of anything distinct, it is a union of love, and is attributed to the Holy Spirit, as a distinct person. And this latter is the most perfect of all, because it approaches nearer than any other to essential union, and is generally the road by which the soul arrives at it.

All these unions are divine *embraces*—but they are not the *Kiss of His mouth.* These unions are of two sorts, the one transitory and very short lived, the other permanent and sustained by the perpetual presence of God, and a sweet and tranquil love, which continues in the midst of everything.

Such, in a few words, is the union of the powers, which is a union of *betrothal;* it implies the affection of the heart, caresses and mutual presents, as is the case with the betrothed, but not the full enjoyment of its object.

Essential union and the kiss of His mouth is the spiritual marriage, where there is a union of essence with essence, and a communication of substance—where God takes the soul for a spouse and unites Himself to it, no longer by persons nor by any act or means, but immediately, reducing all into unity and possessing it in His own unity.

Then it is the *kiss of His mouth,* and real and perfect possession. It is an enjoyment which is neither barren nor unfruitful, since it extends to nothing less than the communication of the Word of God to the soul.

We must remember that God is all *mouth,* as He is all word, and that the application of this divine mouth to the soul is the perfect enjoyment and consummation of the marriage by which the communication of God Himself, and of His word, is made to the soul.

This is what may be called the *apostolic state,* in which the soul is not only *espoused* but *fruitful,* for God, as *mouth,* is some time united to the soul before rendering it fruitful of His own fecundity.

There are some who maintain that this union cannot take place until the next life, but I am confident that it may be attained in this, with this reservation, that here we possess without seeing, there we shall behold what we possess.

Now I say, that while the view of God is in addition to our glory, without which it would be incomplete, it does not, nevertheless, constitute essential beatitude; for we are happy from the moment we receive the supreme Good, and can receive and enjoy it without seeing it. We enjoy it here in the night of faith, where we have the pleasure of enjoyment without the satisfaction of sight; there, we shall have the clear vision of God in addition to the happiness of possessing Him. But this blindness hinders neither the true possession nor the veritable enjoyment of the object, nor the consummation of the divine marriage, any more than it does the real communication of the Word to the soul.

This is far from imaginary, as will be attested by every person of experience.

The present is a proper opportunity to resolve the difficulty of some spiritual persons who think that when the soul is united with God in an essential union, it can no longer speak of Jesus Christ and his interior states, the soul having passed through and left that state. I agree with them entirely, that union to Jesus Christ has preceded for a long time the essential union, since union with Him as a person, took place during the union of the powers; and further, that the union with the God-man Christ Jesus is the first of all, and occurs at the very beginning of the illuminated life. But as regards the communication of the Word to the soul, I say that the soul must first have arrived in God alone, and been there established in essential union, and by the spiritual marriage, before the divine communication can be made to it; as the fruits and products of marriage can only appear after its consummation.

All this is more real than can be expressed; and in the fact that God here possesses the soul *without interruption,* we may trace the difference between essential union and every other kind. When united with the creature, we can only enjoy it by intervals, because the creature is without; but the enjoyment of God is permanent and lasting, because it is within, and God being our final end, the soul can incessantly pour itself into Him as into its goal and centre, to be there mingled and transformed without ever again coming out. Just as a river, which is composed of water derived from the sea, and quite distinct from it, finding itself away from its original, endeavors in various ways to reach the ocean; which, having done, it loses and mixes itself with it, just as it was before it left there, and can no longer be distinguished from it.

It is further to be observed, that God, in creating us, made us *participants* of His being and fit to be reunited to Him; at the same time bestowing upon us a *tendency* towards such a reunion. He has imparted a similar trait to the human body in respect to man in a state of innocence, drawing it from man himself, that He might give it this inclination to union, as to its origin. But as this takes place between gross, material substances, the union can only be material and very restricted, because it occurs between solid and impenetrable bodies. This may be illustrated by the attempt to unite two metals of very different qualities by fusing them together; they never can be perfectly united on account of their dissimilitude; but the nearer alike the two metals are, the more readily they mix. On the other hand, mix two glasses of water, and the two immediately become so mingled as to be undistinguishable. Thus, the soul, being perfectly spiritual in its character, is altogether fitted to be united, mingled and transformed in its God.

This may be illustrated by the union of salt and water: when a lump of rock salt is thrown into water, there is union between the two, because they are on all sides united; but when the salt is liquefied, dissolved and vanished, then there is union and admixture.

There may be a union without any intermixture; such is the union of the powers. But the intermingling is the essential union; and this union is absolute, being of all in the all.

It is only to God that the soul can be thus united, because such is its nature by creation. This is what Saint Paul calls *being changed into the same image* and the Savior, *oneness*.

Now this takes place when the soul loses its proper subsistence to exist only in God; by which is meant mystically, the loss of all self-appropriation, and a loving and perfect sinking of the soul into Him, and not that essential despoiling of its intimate existence implied in the hypostatic union. It is as when a drop of water is let fall into a cup of wine; it loses its own appropriate form and character, and is apparently changed into wine; but its being and substance always remains entirely distinct; so that, if it were the will of God, an Angel could, at any time, separate the identical drop. In the same way, the soul may always be separated from God, though with great difficulty.

This, then, is the lofty and intimate union that the Spouse so pressingly demands at the hand of the Bridegroom. She asks it of Him as though she was addressing another; an impetuous sally of love, giving vent to her passion without particular thought as to whom she was speaking. *Let Him kiss me,* says she, since He can do it, but let it be *with the kisses of His mouth;* no other union can content me; that alone can satisfy all my desires, and that is what I demand.

Verse 1 (continued) to Verse 2. For thy breasts are better than wine, and more fragrant than the choicest ointments.

Thy *breasts,* O God, from which Thou nourishest souls in their beginnings, are so sweet and pleasant, that they render Thy children, and even those who have yet need of the breast, stronger than the stoutest men who are drinkers of *wine.* They are so *fragrant* that, by their charming *perfume,* they attract those souls that are happy enough to perceive it; they are also like a *precious ointment* that heals every interior wound. Ah! if this be so, even at the outset, what delights will there not be in the *nuptial kiss,* the kiss of His mouth!

This Song of Songs starts in the beginning with, an announcement of what is to be its end, and, as it were, the recompense and perfection of the Spouse; for it is altogether natural that the prospect and desire of the end should precede the choice of the means. These latter are then described in order, beginning with spiritual infancy.

It was a view of this end, that induced the Spouse to ask, in the first instance, *the kiss of his mouth;* though it is the last thing she will receive, and that only after having undergone many a trial and many a toil.

Verse 2 (continued). Thy name is as oil poured forth; therefore have the virgins loved thee.

Sensible grace, which is here signified by the *name* of the Bridegroom, penetrates the whole soul so powerfully with the sweetness which God sends to the souls He intends to fill with His love, that it is truly like a *balm poured forth,* which extends and insensibly increases, in proportion as it is more and more poured out, and with so excellent an odor that the young soul finds itself wholly penetrated by its power and sweetness. This takes place without violence, and with so much pleasure that the soul, still *young* and feeble, suffers itself to be carried away by these innocent charms. This is the way God causes Himself to be *loved by young hearts,* who are not as yet capable of loving except on account of the pleasure they experience in loving. It was by a stream of this *oil of gladness,* that the Father anointed the Son above his fellows, who shall share His glory with Him.

Verse 3. Draw me, we will run after thee to the odor of thine ointments.

This young lover prays the Bridegroom to *draw* her by the centre of her soul, as if she were not satisfied with the sweetness of the balsam poured forth among her powers; for she already comprehends, through the grace of the Bridegroom, who continually draws her with more and more force, that there is an enjoyment of Himself more noble and more intimate than that which she at present shares. This is what gives rise to her present request. *Draw me,* says she, into the most interior chambers of my soul, that my powers and senses may all run to Thee by this deeper though less perceptible course. *Draw me,* O divine Lover! *and we will run after Thee* by recollection which causes us to perceive the divine force by which Thou drawest us towards Thee. In running, we will be guided by a certain *odor,* perceived by virtue of Thine attraction which is the smell of the *ointment* Thou hast already poured forth to heal the evil that sin has caused in our powers, and to purify our senses from the corruption that has there entered. We will even outrun this odor to reach Thee, the centre of our bliss.

This excellent *perfume* gives rise to the prayer of recollection, because the senses as well as the powers all *run after* its odor, which causes them to taste with delight *that the Lord is good.*

Verse 3 (continued). The King hath brought me into his store-chambers; we will exult and be glad in thee, remembering thy breasts better than wine; the upright love thee.

The soul has no sooner manifested her desire to pass by all creatures that it may run to Him, than, to recompense her for a love already somewhat purified, He causes her *to enter into his divine store-chambers.* This is a greater grace than any she has hitherto received, for it is a transient union in the powers.

When the heart of a man displays sufficient fidelity to be willing to dispense with all the gifts of God that it may reach God himself, He takes pleasure in showering upon it a profusion of the very gifts it did not seek; but He removes them with indignation from those who prefer them to seeking Himself alone.

It was a knowledge of this, that caused the royal prophet to urge all men *to seek the Lord and His strength; to seek His face evermore*; as though he would have said, do not stop at the graces or gifts of God, which are only as the rays that issue from His face, but which are not Himself; mount up to His very throne and there seek Him; *seek His face evermore* until you are so blessed as to find it.

Then, says the Spouse, transported with joy at the ineffable secret revealed to her, then, when we are in thee, O God, *we shall exult and be glad in Thee; we will remember thy breasts more than wine;* that is, the remembrance of having preferred the Bridegroom over everything else, will be the height of her joy and pleasure. She had already chosen the sweetness of his milk before the wine of the pleasures of this world; wherefore, she says, *we will remember thy breasts more than wine.* Here she chooses God in preference to His spiritual consolations; and the transports of grace, which she experienced while drawing the milk of His breasts.

She adds, *the upright love Thee,* to signify that the true uprightness which leads the soul to dispense with all the pleasures of earth and the enjoyments of heaven, to be lost in God, is what constitutes pure and perfect love. In truth, O my God, none but those who are *upright* in the way, can *love* Thee as Thou deservest to be loved!

Verse 4. I am black, but comely, O ye daughters of Jerusalem, as the tents of Kedar, as the curtains of Solomon.

As the greatest graces of God tend always to produce in us a deeper knowledge of what we are, and as they would not come from Him, if they did not give, in their degree, a certain taste of the misery of the creature, so it is with this soul; scarcely has she emerged from the store chambers of the King before she discovers that she is *black.* What is this thy blackness, O thou incomparable maiden? (we say to her;) tell us, we pray thee. *I am black,* she says, because I perceive by the light of my divine Sun, hosts of defects, of which I was never aware until now; I am black, because I am not yet cleansed of self.

But, nevertheless, I am *comely as the tents of Kedar;* for this experimental knowledge of what I am, is extremely pleasing to my Bridegroom, and induces Him to visit me as a place of rest. I am comely, because, having no voluntary stain, my Spouse renders me fair with His own beauty. The blacker I am in my own eyes, the fairer I am in His.

I am comely, too, *as the curtains of Solomon,* The curtains of the divine Solomon are the holy Humanity, which conceals the Word of God made flesh. I am comely, she says, as His *curtains,* for He has made me a partaker of His beauty in this, that as the holy Humanity concealed the Divinity, so my apparent blackness hides the greatness of God's workings in my soul.

I am *black* also from the crosses and persecutions which attack me from without; but I *am comely as the curtains of Solomon,* because blackness and the cross make me like Him.

I am *black* because outward weaknesses appear in me, but I am comely, because my intention is pure within.

Verse 5. Look not upon me because I am dark-colored, because the sun hath tanned me; my mother's children strove against me; they made me keeper in the vineyards; but mine own vineyard have I not kept.

Why is it that the betrothed asks *that they will not look upon her* in her blackness? Because the soul, entering now into the state of faith, and spoliation of sensible grace, loses by degrees the sweet vigor that led her so easily to the practice of virtue, and made her externally so beautiful. And not being able any longer to perform, her previous acts, because God requires something else of her, she seems to have fallen back into a state of nature.

This seems so to those who are not enlightened, and it is for this reason that she exclaims: I beseech you, my friends and companions, who have not yet arrived at so interior a point, you, who are yet in the first experiences of the spiritual life, judge me not because I am dark colored externally, nor because of my outward defects, real or apparent; for they do not happen from want of love and courage, as is the case with souls in the beginning, but because my divine Sun has looked upon me with his constant, burning beams, and changed my color. He has taken away my natural complexion that I might have only such a one as his fiery fervor would give me. It is the violence of love that dries up and tans my skin, and not its departure. This blackness is an advance, not a relapse; but a progress not for your imitation at your tender age, for the blackness which you would give yourselves would be a defect; to be right it must only proceed from the Sun of Righteousness, who, for His own glory and the highest good of the soul, burns up and destroys that dazzling outward complexion which was a source of blindness to the soul, though a cause of great admiration to those about, to the great prejudice of the Bridegroom's glory.

My mother's children beholding me thus *black,* sought to *compel* me to resume my active life, and direct my attention to the exterior, instead of devoting myself to the destruction of my interior passions; they strove against me for a long while, and in the end, not being able to resist them, I yielded to their desires; but in attending to these outward and foreign things, *I have not kept mine own vineyard,* which is my interior, where my God dwells. That is my whole care, and the only vineyard I ought to keep; and since I have not kept mine own; since I have been inattentive to the voice of my God, I have been still less faithful in guarding those of others. This is the persecution that souls are ordinarily subjected to, when it is once perceived that their constant introversion causes neglect of some external thing, the soul being entirely turned inward, and hence not being able to apply herself to the correction of certain trifling defects that the Bridegroom will Himself remedy in due time.

Verse 6. Tell me, O thou whom my soul loveth, where thou feedest, where thou reposest at midday, lest I should begin to wander after the flocks of thy companions.

O Thou whom my soul loveth! exclaims this poor affianced one, thus obliged to leave the sweet employment within, to be engaged about external matters of the lowest description; O Thou, whom I love so much the more as I find my love more thwarted; ah, show me *where Thou feedest Thy flocks,* and with what food Thou satisfiest the souls that are so blessed as to be under Thy care! We know that when Thou wert upon earth, *Thy meat and drink was to do the will of Thy Father,* and now Thy meat is that Thy friends do Thy will. Thou still feedest Thy followers upon Thyself, revealing to them Thine infinite perfection, to the end that they may love Thee more fervently; and the more Thou art revealed, the more they seek to know, that they may be able ever to love Thee more and more.

Tell me also, pursues she, *where Thou reposest at noon!* By this figure she intends to convey the vehemence of pure love desiring to learn from its author and master, in what it consists; lest perchance, wandering into some human path, though under the semblance of spirituality, she may be misled, and may be ministering to self-love, at the very moment when she was persuaded she had nothing in view, but pure love and the glory of God alone.

She is right in fearing a mistake which involves such important consequences, and which is too common among the flocks of the church. It happens whenever persons are guided by spiritual advisers whom Jesus Christ has truly rendered His companions, associating them with Himself in the direction of souls, but who, not being dead to themselves nor crucified to the world with Him, do not teach their pupils to deny themselves; to be crucified and dead in everything, in order to live to God only, and that Christ may live in them. Whence it happens, that both being in an extremely natural and unmortified life, their path is also exceedingly human, and consequently liable to turn aside hither and thither, frequently changing their devotions and their guides, without ever arriving at anything solid. And because this wandering arises from the failure to consult with care the maxims and example of Jesus Christ, and to apply to Him by prayer to obtain from Him what He alone can grant us, therefore it is that this beloved soul, being well instructed, implores with so much earnestness the knowledge of His Word with which He feeds souls, and faithfulness to follow his example. For she knows that these alone, with the help of grace, can prevent her from going astray.

We are too often arrested at created means, however religious. God alone can teach us to do His will, for He alone is our God.

She asks also of the Word that He would conduct her to his Father, since He is the way that leads there. The bosom of the Father being the place where He rests in the noontide of His glory, and in the full light of eternity, she desires to be lost in God with Jesus His Son; to be there hidden and there to rest forever. And though she does not say so explicitly, she gives us to understand it distinctly enough by what she says afterwards,—*lest I should begin to wander* as I have done. There I shall be perfectly secure; I shall never more be deceived; and what is far better, I shall sin no more.

Verse 7. If thou know not, O thou fairest among women, go thy way forth by the footsteps of the flock, and feed thy kids beside the shepherds' tents.

The Bridegroom replies to His Bride, and to prepare her for the grace which He would bestow, as well as to instruct her in the use of what she has already received, He gives her a most important direction—*If thou know not,* says He, *go forth.* He means to say that she cannot know the divine object of her love, however passionately she may desire it, except she first know herself; for the nothingness of the creature helps our conception of the *all* of God. But as the light necessary for discovering the creature's abyss of nothingness exists only in the all of God, He directs her to *go forth.* Whence? From herself. How? By abandonment and fidelity in applying it to everything, permitting herself no natural satisfaction and no life in self or any creature. And whither? To enter into God by an absolute self-abandonment, where she will find that He is *all and in all*; and that she herself, consequently, and every creature, are merely nothingness.

Now, nothingness deserves no esteem, because it has no good; neither does it merit love, for it is nothing; it is only worthy, on the contrary, of contempt and hatred on account of the self-esteem and self-love entirely opposed to God, that have been implanted in it by sin. If the creature, then, aspire to Divine Union, it must be well persuaded of the all of God and its own nothingness, and must go forth of itself, feeling nothing but contempt and hatred for itself, that it may reserve all its esteem and love for God; and by this means, it may attain to union.

This *going forth from self* by a perpetual abandonment of every selfish interest, is the interior work which the Heavenly Bridegroom prescribes to those who are sighing after the kiss of His mouth. He thus signifies it to this soul by the single expression, *go forth,* which is sufficient to guide her inward course.

As regards the outward, it is His will that she should neglect no part of her duty in the station in which He has placed her, a direction which comprehends infinitely more than the most minute detail could do, and while she must follow the attraction of the Holy Spirit in all liberty as to the inward life, He would have her also conform to the external usages of religion and be obedient to those in authority, as to the exterior, and this He expresses by *going forth in the footsteps of the flock,* that is to say, in the ordinary, common way, externally, and by *feeding the kids,*—that is, the senses—by the shepherds' tents.

Verse 8. I have compared thee, O my love, to my company of horsemen in Pharaoh's chariots.

The Bridegroom knowing perfectly well that all the commendations which He lavishes on His beloved, far from rendering her vain, only further her annihilation, praises her in magnificent strains, that her love may be fed. *I have compared thee,* he says, *to My company of horsemen;* that is, I desire of thee a course so swift and sure in Me that I can only liken thy single soul to a whole company running toward Me with extreme rapidity; I have compared thee to My angels, and I will for thee the same bliss that they enjoy, *always to behold My face.*

Still, for the better concealment of such great things while thou art upon the earth, I have made thee externally like to the chariots of Pharaoh. Those who behold thee running so swiftly and as it were disorderly, will believe that thou art in search of the pleasures, the vanities and the multiplicities of Egypt, or that thou art busy in self-seeking in such eager haste, but thou art running toward Me, and thy race shall end in Me alone, and nothing shall prevent thy safe arrival, because of the strength and fidelity with which I have supplied thee.

Verse 9. Thy cheeks are comely as a turtle dove's; thy neck as jewels.

The cheeks signify the interior and exterior; *they are comely as a turtle dove's.* The dove is said to have this peculiarity, that when one of a pair dies, the other ever after remains single, without seeking another mate. So the soul, separated from its God, can take no pleasure in any creature, either within or without. Within, it is reduced to a solitude so much the more complete, in that, not finding the Bridegroom, it cannot be occupied with anything else. Without, everything is dead, so far as it is concerned; and it is this very separation of the soul from every creature and from everything that is not God, that constitutes its beauty in the eyes of the Well-beloved.

Her neck represents pure love, which is the greatest stay left her. But though she appears in a state of the greatest nakedness, she is still enriched by the practice of numberless virtues, which, like *jewels* of great price, serve as an ornament. But without this adornment, love alone would render her perfectly beautiful, just as the neck of the bride, though stripped of jewels, is not deprived of beauty.

Verse 10. We will make thee chains of gold inlaid with silver.

Although thou art already very beautiful in thy nakedness, the evidence of a pure heart and unfeigned charity; we will still add something farther to set off thy beauty, by giving thee precious ornaments. These shall be *chains,* in token of thy perfect submission to every will of the King of Glory. But they shall be of *gold,* to signify that, acting only from an exceedingly purified love, thou hast but a single and pure regard to the good pleasure and glory of God in everything thou doest or sufferest for Him. Nevertheless, they shall be *inlaid with silver;* because, however simple and pure charity may be in itself, it must appear and be made manifest externally, in the practice of good works and the most excellent virtues.

It is to be noted, that the Divine Master takes special care in many passages to instruct His beloved pupil as to the supreme purity He requires in the love of the Spouse, and in her faithfulness to neglect nothing in the service of the Well-beloved, or the help of the neighbor.

Verse 11. While the King was reclining upon his couch, my spikenard sent forth the smell thereof.

The Spouse is not yet so unclothed but that she receives from time to time visits from her Well-beloved. But why do I call it a visit? It is rather a manifestation of Himself, an experience of His deep and central presence. The holy Bridegroom is ever in the centre of the soul that is faithful to Him; but He often dwells there in such a hidden manner, that the

Spouse is almost always ignorant of her happiness except at certain times, when He is pleased to reveal Himself to the loving soul, which then perceives Him deeply and intimately present. Such is His conduct toward this the purest of His followers, as is testified by her words *when my King,* He who reigns over and guides me as a Sovereign, *was reclining upon His couch,* which is the ground and centre of my soul, where He takes His rest; *my spikenard,* that is, my faithfulness, *sent forth the smell thereof* so sweetly and pleasantly, that He was obliged to discover Himself to me. Then I recognized that He was reposing within me as on His royal couch, which before I was ignorant of, for although He was there, yet I knew it not.

Verse 12. A bundle of myrrh is my well-beloved unto me; he shall abide between my breasts.

When the Bride, or rather the lover (for she is not yet a bride), has found her Bridegroom, she is so transported with joy, that she is eager to be instantly united to Him. But the union of perpetual enjoyment is not yet arrived. He is *mine,* she says, I cannot doubt that He gives Himself to me this moment, since I feel it, but He is to me, as it were, a *bundle of myrrh.* He is not yet a Bridegroom whom I may embrace in the nuptial bed, but a bundle of crosses, pains and mortifications; a bloody husband, and crucified lover, who desires to test my faithfulness, by making me partaker of a good share of his sufferings. For this is the part of the soul at this period.

As an evidence, however, of the progress of this already heroic soul, note that she does not say, my

Well-beloved will give me the bundle of the cross, but
that He Himself should be that bundle; for all my
crosses shall be those of my Well-beloved. This
bundle shall be *betwixt my breasts* as an evidence that
He will be a Bridegroom of bitterness as well without
as within. External crosses are a small matter, if
unaccompanied by those which are internal, and the
inward are rendered much more painful by the
simultaneous presence of the outward. But though
the soul perceives nothing but the cross on every
side, it is nevertheless her Well-beloved in the shape
of the cross, and He never is more present to her than
in those seasons of bitterness, during which He
dwells in the midst of her heart.

Verse 13. My beloved is unto me as a cluster of cypress, in the
vineyards of Engaddi.

My beloved, continues the lover, *is unto me as a
cluster of cypress.* She only partially expresses herself;
it is as though she said: He is only near to me, for I
have not the blessedness of that intimate union by
which He would dwell wholly in me, and I in Him. He
is nevertheless near to me but *as a cluster of cypress*
(a shrub producing a very fragrant balm), since it is
He only who gives odor and value to everything that
is done by those who love Him. This cluster grows *in
the vineyards of Engaddi,* which are very beautiful,
and the grapes of which are excellent. She compares
her Well-beloved to the pleasant fragrance and
excellent virtue of balsam, to the delight and strength
of wine, to express by these images that he, who has
learned from the interior enjoyment of God to put his
pleasure in Him, can no longer find delight in
anything else; and that we no sooner seek any other

source of satisfaction than we lose that which is divine.

The Well-beloved beholding the readiness of the Spouse to be crucified and instructed by Him, is charmed with the lustre of the beauty He has bestowed upon her. He caresses and praises her, calling her His fair one and His well-beloved.— *Behold, thou art fair, my love,* He says, *behold, thou art fair!*— Sweet words! He refers to a double beauty, one external, the other internal; but He desires that she should perceive it, as though He would say: Behold, thou art fair already in the depths, though thou art not yet perfected; know, too, that in a little while thou shalt be perfectly beautiful without, when I shall have finished thee and drawn thee out of thy weaknesses.

These praises are accompanied by the promise of a more exquisite beauty, in the hope of which the soul will take courage, while its humility is cherished by reflecting on its imperfections.

But why does He say that in a little while she shall be endued with a double beauty? It is because she has already *doves' eyes;* that is, she is simple within, not turning aside from the view of her God, and without, in all her words and actions, which are destitute of guile.

This dove-like simplicity is the surest mark of the advancement of a soul; for no longer making use of indirect means or artifices, she is led by the Spirit of God. The Spouse understood from the beginning the necessity of simplicity and the perfect nature of uprightness when she said, *the upright love Thee;* (verse 3), where she places the perfection of love in its simplicity and uprightness.

Verse 15. Behold, thou art fair, my beloved, and comely; our bed is adorned with flowers.

The loving soul seeing that her Bridegroom has praised her for her double beauty, and unwilling to appropriate anything to herself, says in return, *Behold, Thou art fair, my beloved, and comely.* She returns Him all the praise she had received from Him, and adds more on her own part. Nothing belonging to us, no praise, no glory, and no pleasure, everything must be referred to Him who is the author and centre of every good. The loving soul teaches us this important point of practice throughout, everywhere giving glory to the Lord for everything He has bestowed upon her. If I am beautiful, she says to Him, it is with Thine own beauty; it is Thou who art beautiful in me with this double beauty, which Thou praisest in me.

Our bed, she adds, that inner retreat in which Thou dwellest in me, and which I call *ours,* that Thou mayst thereby be induced to come and give me there the nuptial kiss which I first asked of Thee, and which is my final end—our bed is ready, and *adorned with the flowers* of a thousand virtues.

Verse 16. The beams of our houses are of cedar and our carved ceilings are of cypress.

The Bridegroom, hidden in the ground and centre of the soul (as has been said), takes pleasure in sending from the sanctuary in which He dwells, certain effusions of His sensible graces, which produce, in the exterior of the Spouse, an abundance of different virtues, which are like flowers. Finding herself adorned with these she is so surprised and charmed, or perhaps has so little experience, that she believes her inward edifice is nearly completed. The roof is on, she says; *the beams,* which are the practice of exterior virtues, *are laid of cedar;* methinks I perceive their agreeable odor and that I can practice them with as much strength as ease. The regulation of the senses appears to me to be perfectly accomplished as the setting in order of the carved and beautiful *ceiling of cypress.*

But, O Spouse! this only appears so to thee because thy bed is adorned with flowers, and because the sweet, grateful and pleasant state which thou experiencest within, makes thee believe that thou hast gained everything without; but remember, thy *ceilings* are of *cypress,* which is a tree of death, and all this beauty and adornment are but the preparation for a sacrifice.

CHAPTER 2

VERSE 1. I am the flower of the field, and the lily of the valleys.

THIS, O my God, is a gentle reproach of my Spouse for desiring so soon to repose upon a flowery couch, before having rested with Thee upon the painful bed of the cross. *I am the flower of the field,* He says, a flower you will not find in the repose of the couch, but which must be culled in the field of combat, labor and suffering. I am the *lily of the valleys,* which only grows in annihilated souls. If, then, you would have me uproot you from earth that I may take root in you, you must be in the extremest annihilation; if you would find me, you must engage in combat and endure hardship.

Verse 2. As the lily among thorns, so is my love among the daughters.

By these words the Bridegroom signifies the progress of his beloved, since she is like a lily, very pure and pleasant, and of a sweet odor before Him; while the other daughters, instead of being docile and pliable, and suffering themselves to be fed by his Spirit, are like a thicket of thorns which is impenetrable, and wounds those who attempt to approach it. Such are souls self-possessed and immersed in their own wills, who refuse to be guided towards God. And this is a cause of suffering to an abandoned soul when placed among such; for they do all that lies in their power to draw her out of the way; but as the lily perfectly preserves both its purity and its perfume even when surrounded by *thorns,* so these souls are preserved by the Bridegroom, in the midst of the opposition which they experience from those who prefer to be their own guides and to dwell in the multiplicity of their own works, having no docility in following the movement of grace.

Verse 3. As the appletree among the trees of the wood, so is my beloved among the sons. I sat down under the shadow of him whom I desired, and his fruit was sweet to my taste.

How much simplicity is there in this comparison! The beloved beholding herself persecuted by such spiritual persons as do not understand her experience, addresses herself to them and to her Well-beloved at the same time. *As the appletree among the trees of the wood, so is my beloved among the sons;* that is, among those most pleasing in the sight of God, whether saints in heaven or the righteous upon the earth. Be not surprised, then, if *I sit down under His shadow,* and remain at rest under His protection. I am only under the shadow of the wings of Him by whom I have greatly desired to be possessed; and although I have not yet arrived at so desirable an attainment, yet I can say that *His fruit—*

that is, crosses, pain and abasement—*is sweet to my taste.* It is not sweet to the taste of the flesh; for the inferior part finds it bitter and ill-flavored; but it is sweet to the mouth of the heart, after it is once swallowed, and by me, whose taste is that of my Well-beloved, it is more to be desired than all other delights.

Verse 4. He brought me into the wine cellars and set love in order within me.

The beloved of the King, issuing from her delightful interviews with Him, appears to her companions to be intoxicated and beside herself. She is so in truth; for having tasted of the finest *wine* of the Bridegroom, she could not help being seized with the extremest ardor. Being quite sensible of it herself, she begs her companions not to be amazed at seeing her in so extraordinary a condition; my intoxication, she says, is excusable, for my King has *brought me into his divine wine cellars,* and there *has set love in order within me.* The first time He made me partaker of such singular grace, I was so feeble that I would rather have preferred the sweetness of the divine breasts to the strength of this excellent wine, and therefore He was content to show me its effects, suffering me to drink but little of it. But now that experience and His grace have rendered me wiser and stronger, I can no longer do so; I have drunk so abundantly of His strong and pure wine, that He has set love in order within me.

What *order* is this that God ordains in love? O Love! O God of Charity! Thou alone canst reveal it! He causes this soul, who by a movement of charity desired for herself every possible good in reference to God, to forget herself wholly that she may only think upon her Well-beloved. She becomes divested of every selfish interest in her own salvation, perfection, joy, or consolation, that she may only think of the interests of God. She no longer thinks of enjoying His embrace, but of suffering for Him. She no longer asks anything for herself, but only that He may be glorified. She enters fully into the designs of the divine righteousness, consenting with all her heart to everything it decrees with respect to her and in her, whether for time or eternity. She can love nothing in herself or in any creature except in and for God, and not in and for self, however important and necessary it may appear.

Such is the order of charity which God ordains in this soul; her love is become perfectly chaste. All creatures are nothing to her; she wills them only for her God, and none of them for herself. Ah! what strength does this well ordered charity impart for the terrible states that are to follow! But it can only be known and enjoyed of those who have experienced it; the others have not yet tasted of the Bridegroom's wine.

Verse 5. Stay me with flowers, strew me with apples; for I am sick of love.

The Bridegroom has no sooner thus ordered charity in the soul, than He bestows upon her peculiar grace to prepare her for the sufferings that are to succeed. He gives her His transitory union in the centre, which from there expands into the senses and powers. And as she is not yet very strong, there is, as it were, an absorption or suspension of the senses which forces her to cry out, *Stay me with flowers,* help me with some little external practices, or *strew me with apples,* some of the fruits of the exercise of charity, that I die not under these powerful charms. *For,* I perceive that *I am sick of love.* Poor child! what sayest thou? Why talk of being comforted by flowers and fruits, exterior consolations—trifles? Thou knowest not what thou askest; forgive my plainness. If thou faintest under this trial, thou fallest only into the arms of thy loved one! and happy wouldst thou be to expire there! But thou art not yet prepared for this.

Verse 6. His left hand is under my head, and his right hand shall embrace me.

She begins to understand the mystery, and, repenting of the foreign support she had sought, she says, *His left hand is under my head;* He bears me up with singular care, since He has honored me with union with Himself in the powers of my soul. What business, then, have I with flowers and fruits, that is, with things sensible and human, since He favors me with those which are divine? He is even going on to do more for me, uniting me to Himself in essence, and I shall then be fruitful and produce for my Bridegroom fruits incomparably more beautiful than those I desired, for *He will embrace me with His right hand,* which is His omnipotence accompanied by His love, the chaste embraces of which produce in the soul the perfect enjoyment of Him, which is only another name for essential union.

It is true that at first, this embrace of the right hand is the affiancing of the soul, but not its marriage. *He will embrace me,* she says; He will first bind me to Himself by the tie of betrothal, by which I have the hope of a future marriage, when He will so embrace me and so bind me to Himself that I shall fear no subsequent defection. For the peculiarity of essential union is to strengthen the soul so fully, that it no longer suffers those faintings which beset souls in their beginnings, who, grace being as yet feeble in them, experience eclipses and falls. In this state, the soul is confirmed in love, since it then dwells in God; *and he who dwells in God, dwells in love;* for God is love.

Verse 7. I charge you, O ye daughters of Jerusalem, by the roes and by the hinds of the field, that ye stir not up, nor awake my love till she please.

The soul is in a mystic slumber in this embrace of betrothal, in which she enjoys a sacred rest she had never before experienced. In her previous intervals of repose, she had indeed rested under His shadow by her confidence in Him, but she had never slept upon His bosom nor in His arms. It is strange how eager the creatures are, even those which are spiritual, to awake the soul from this gentle slumber. The *daughters of Jerusalem* are loving and meddlesome souls, who are anxious to wake her, though under the most specious pretexts; but she is so soundly asleep that she cannot be aroused. Then the Bridegroom speaks for her, and clasping her in his arms, *charges* them by what they esteem the most highly, the practice of the most impetuous and active virtues, *not to awake His love,* nor disturb her repose, for she is more pleasing to Him in this rest, than she would be in all her external activity. Wake her not, He says, neither directly or indirectly, nor use any far-fetched ingenuity to accomplish your purpose; let her rest, *until she please,* for she will please, whenever I please.

Verse 8. The voice of my beloved! behold, he cometh, leaping upon the mountains, skipping upon the hills.

The soul, asleep to everything else, is only the more attentive to the voice of her Well- beloved; she hears and recognizes it at once.

The voice of my Beloved! she says I know it, I hear it, and its effects upon me removes all my doubts. But what sayest thou, O beloved one? Thou wert perchance dreaming from love; asleep in the arms of thy Bridegroom, thou yet seest Him, *leaping upon the mountains and skipping upon the hills!* How then can this be? The Bridegroom embraces his beloved and dwells in her. He surrounds her without and penetrates her within; she feels that, in this mystic slumber, he enters more deeply and becomes united to her, not only as heretofore, in the powers which are *the hills,* but in a much superior degree; He comes upon *the mountains,* that is, the centre, and there He touches her truly with his immediate union. She at once perceives that this influence is far different from that in the powers, and that it is the cause of very great effects, though it is but a transitory touch and not a permanent and lasting union.

Verse 9. My beloved is like a roe or a young hart: behold he standeth behind our wall; he looketh forth at the windows, showing himself through the lattice.

While the soul is thus receiving the sweet caresses of the Bridegroom, she thinks they will last forever; but if they are the pledges of His love, they are also the tokens of His departure. Scarcely has she begun to taste the pleasantness of union before He is wholly gone, and she compares His rapid disappearance to the movements of *a roe or a young hart.* While she is fondly lamenting his strange abandonment of her and when she thought Him far distant, she suddenly perceives Him *close at hand.* He had only hid Himself to try her faith and confidence in Him; but he never removes *His look* from her, protecting her more carefully than ever, being more closely united to her than ever before by the new union that has just taken place. But although He always beholds her, she does not always see Him. She only perceives Him occasionally, that she may not be ignorant of his watchfulness, and that she may one day teach it to others. It is to be observed, that He *standeth,* since it is now no time to rest, nor even to be seated, but to run; He therefore stands, as if ready to depart.

Verse 10. Behold, my beloved speaketh to me and saith: Rise up, my love, my dove, my fair one, and come.

God having wholly turned the soul within and brought it to its centre, after having caused it to enjoy His chaste embrace to dispose it for its spiritual marriage; He causes it to take a road to all appearance totally opposite, He brings it out of itself by the mystical death. The Well-beloved coming in person to address the soul, invites it to go forth of itself in haste; He no longer bids it take its rest, but commands it to *rise up*. This is very different from His former conduct, then He forbade anyone from waking her, now He would have her rise up at once. He calls her so sweetly and so forcibly, that if she were not as eagerly bent upon doing His will as she is, she could not resist. *Rise up, my love,* whom I have chosen for My bride, *my fair one,* for I find thee lovely, reflecting a thousand traits of My own beauty. Rise up, *My dove,* simple and faithful, and come forth, for thou hast all the necessary qualities for leaving thyself. Having led thee deeply within, I have come out of thee that I may oblige thee, in following Me, to come forth of thyself also.

This coming forth is far other than the one before alluded to (chap. 1 verse 7), and much farther advanced, for the first was but a leaving of natural gratifications, that she might please her Well-beloved, but this is a departure from the possession of self, that she may be possessed by God only, and that, perceiving herself no more in self, she may be found in Him alone.—It is a transportation of the creature into its original, as will be shown by and by.

Verse 11. For lo! the winter is past, the rain is over and gone.

There are two *winters,* one external, the other internal, and these two are reciprocally opposed. When it is winter without, it is summer within, by which the soul is induced to enter more deeply into itself, by an effect of grace operating a profound state of recollection. When it is winter within, it is summer without, thus obliging the soul to come forth from self by the enlargement produced by a more abundant grace of abandonment. *The winter* of which the

Bridegroom here speaks, declaring that it *is past,* is the outward winter, during which the soul might have been frozen by the excessive cold, wet through by the rains, and overwhelmed by the tempests and snows of sins and imperfections, so easily contracted in commerce with the creature. The soul that has found its centre becomes so strong that it has nothing further to fear from without, the rains are dried up, and it would be impossible for it, without being guilty of the blackest infidelity, to take pleasure in anything external.

This expression, *the winter is past,* signifies, too, that as winter brings death to everything, so in this soul death has passed upon all outward things, so that there is none among them that could now satisfy it. If anything should appear to give it pleasure, it is only a return to its state of innocence in which there is no venom as there was before.

The winter *rains are over and gone,* also, she may go out without fear of the weather, and with this additional advantage, that the cold has destroyed what, to her, was formerly alive and would have destroyed her, as the rigor of winter delivers the earth from vermin.

Verse 12. The flowers have appeared on the earth; the pruning time is come, and the voice of the turtle is heard in our land.

To compel her to come forth, He gives her to understand that He is about to lead her into His grounds; He calls them *our land,* because He has acquired them for her by His redemption, and they belong to Him for her, and to her through Him. He says that *the flowers have appeared* there, but they are flowers that never fade, and that fear the coming of winter no more.

The time of pruning the vine has come; the Spouse, who has compared herself to a vine, must now be pruned, cut down, stripped and destroyed.

The voice of the turtle, of My humanity, invites thee to lose and hide thyself with it, in the bosom of My Father, thou wilt hear that voice to more advantage than now, when thou shalt have come to *the land,* whither I call thee, which as yet thou knowest not. This voice of My simplicity and innocence with which I will satisfy thee, is very different from thine.

Verse 13. The figtree hath put forth her green figs, and the flowering vines give a good smell. Arise my love, my fair one, come.

There the spring is eternal, and is accompanied, at the same time, without incongruity, by the fruits of autumn and the heats of summer. The Bridegroom, by these flowers and fruits, points out three distinct seasons; but He no longer refers to winter, for, as has been already stated, when the soul arrives in this new land, she finds that not only the outward but the inward winter also is past.

To the soul that has reached God, there is no longer any winter; but there is a season composed of the other three joined in one, which is, as it were, immortalized by the death of winter. For, before reaching the inner winter, the soul had passed through all the seasons of the spiritual life; but afterward, it re-enters upon a perpetual spring, summer and autumn. The mildness of spring does not prevent the fervor of summer nor the fruitfulness of autumn; the heats of summer do not interfere with the beauty of spring nor the abundance of autumn, and the fruits of autumn interpose no obstacle to the enjoyment of spring, nor to the ardor of summer.

O blessed Land! happy they who are enabled to possess you! We are all entreated, with the Spouse, to come out of self that we may enter there. It is promised to all, and He who possesses it, and to whom it belongs by right of His eternal generation and of the purchase of His blood, earnestly invites us all to proceed thither. He furnishes us with all the means of doing so; He draws us by His urgent solicitations; why do we not make haste?

Verse 14. My dove in the clefts of the rock, in the hollow of the wall, show me thy countenance and let thy voice sound in mine ears; for sweet is thy voice, and thy countenance is comely.

My dove, says the Bridegroom, my pure, chaste and harmless dove, who art ensconced in thyself as in the *hollow of a wall,* and who art there hidden in my wounds, which are *the clefts of the living rock, show me thy countenance.* But why sayest Thou so, O Bridegroom? is not Thy beloved wholly turned towards Thee? Why then dost Thou beg for a sight of her countenance? She is, as it were, wholly hidden in Thee, and dost Thou not behold her? Thou wouldst *hear her voice,* and she is dumb for every other but Thee!

O admirable invention of Divine Wisdom! the poor soul, thinking that to correspond to her

Bridegroom she must continue, as formerly, to recollect herself, and sink still deeper within, endeavors to do so with all her strength; but the contrary is what is required. He here calls her without, and desires that she should leave herself, and for this reason He says, *show me thy countenance, let thy voice sound in Mine ears* without; turn towards Me, for I have moved My place. He assures her that *her voice is sweet,* calm and tranquil; that in that respect she is like her beloved, whose voice is not one that is heard by reason of loud speaking; *thy countenance,* He adds, *is comely;* the superior part of thy soul is already fair and has all the advantages of beauty; there is but one thing wanting; come forth!

If He did not thus sweetly and forcibly draw the soul without, she would never leave herself. It would seem that she now finds herself drawn outward with as much force as she formerly felt herself recollected and impelled inward, and even with greater; for it requires much more power to draw the soul out of self than to sink it within. The sweetness she experiences in her savory recollection, is a sufficient inducement, but to leave this enjoyment within, to find nothing but bitterness without, is a very difficult matter. Besides, by recollection she lives and possesses herself; but by issuing forth from self, she perishes and dies.

Verse 15. Take us the little foxes that spoil the vines; for our vine is in blossom.

The faithful soul prays her beloved that He will *take* away *the little foxes,* which are numerous little defects that begin to appear; for they *spoil* the interior *vine,* which, she says, *is in blossom.* It is for this reason very delightful to her, and the more so as she expects soon to enjoy the ripe fruit.

How wilt thou be able, poor soul, to abandon this vine to which thou art so attached, without being aware of it? Ah! the Master himself will permit the little foxes to spoil it, destroy the flowers and make strange havoc with it! Were He not to do this, thou art so in love with thyself, that thou wouldst never come forth.

Verse 16. My beloved is mine and I am his; he feedeth among the lilies.

O inconceivable happiness of a soul wholly and unreservedly devoted to her *beloved,* and to whom the Well-beloved is all! The Spouse is here so enamored of the goodness and caresses of the Bridegroom manifested for the purpose of obliging her to leave herself, that she thinks she has already arrived at the height of felicity and summit of perfection, and that her marriage is now to take place. She says that her Beloved is hers, to dispose of as pleases Him, and that she is His, for the whole extent of His will; that *He feeds among the lilies* of her purity. He feeds upon His own graces and virtues; He lives upon innocence and purity, that He may nourish us with the same. He invites us to eat with Him the meat He likes the best, as He gives us to understand by these words in another place: *Eat, O friends; drink, yea, drink abundantly, O beloved! Hearken diligently unto me and eat ye that which is good, and let your soul delight itself in fatness.*

Verse 17. Until the day break and the shadows flee away, turn, my beloved, and be thou like a roe or a young hart upon the mountains of Bether.

The soul, beginning to be conscious that she no longer perceives the Word, believes that He is only hidden for a night, or rather, that He is sleeping in His place of rest. She says to Him, O my Beloved, since I am under the same roof with Thee and Thou art so near me, *turn* a little towards me, that I may perceive Thee! Let me enjoy the delights of Thy society *until the day break*, and I may have further evidence of Thy presence; until *the shadows of faith flee* away and yield to the soft light of vision and unclouded enjoyment! Then, remembering the transitory union which she formerly experienced, she cries: Run quickly, if it seem good to Thee, *like a roe or a young hart* that bounds, but let it be *upon the mountains;* let me once more enjoy that central union, that was so sweet and profitable when it was granted me before.

CHAPTER 3

VERSE 1. By night on my bed, I sought him whom my soul loveth; I sought him but I found him not.

THE SOUL, finding that the Bridegroom does not grant her a favor which she surely counted on, as he had formerly bestowed it when she did not hope for it, is astonished at his prolonged absence. *She seeks Him* in her interior, which is *her bed,* and *during the night* of faith, but alas! she is sadly surprised *not to find Him!* She had some reason to seek Him there, since it was there that He discovered Himself to her, and gave her the liveliest conception which she had yet experienced of His character.

But, O Spouse! thou canst not find Him there! Knowest thou not, that He bade thee seek Him no longer in thee but in Himself? Thou wilt not now find Him anywhere out of Himself. Depart from self in all haste that thou mayest be no longer but in Him, and there thou wilt find Him! O wonderful stratagem of the Bridegroom! When he is most enamored of His

Well-beloved, He flies from her with the greatest
cruelty; but it is cruelty full of love, and without it the
soul would never depart from self, and consequently
would never be lost in God.

Verse 2. I will rise now and go about the city in the streets, and in
the broad ways I will seek him whom my soul loveth: sought him,
but I found him not.

Behold a miracle performed by the absence of a
God! How many times had He invited His beloved to
rise from her repose, and she could not do it? He
entreated her with the tenderest expressions, but she
was so intoxicated with the peace and tranquillity
which she enjoyed, that she could not be induced to
leave them.

O faithful soul! the repose enjoyed in thyself is
but a shadow of that which thou wilt find in God! But
it was impossible to arouse her; but now that she no
longer finds her Well-beloved in her resting place, O,
she exclaims, *I will rise now;* this couch, which was
once paradise to me, is now a hell, since my beloved
is gone; and with Him hell would be a paradise.

The city, this world which I formerly hated, shall
be the field of *my seeking.* The soul, not yet fully
instructed, however enamored she may appear, and
justly eager for the possession of the Bridegroom, her
final end, yet here talks as a child. She is so weak, that
she cannot at first seek God in Himself; although she
does not find Him within herself, she must seek Him
in *every* creature, in a thousand places where He is
not, and being thus dispersed abroad, she is occupied
with the creature under pretext of seeking the
Creator. *She seeks,* nevertheless; for her heart loves

and can find no rest but in the object of its love, but *she finds nothing,* because God has not departed from her to be sought in other creatures. He desires to be sought in Himself, and when she shall have arrived there she will discover another truth, the beauty of which will entrance her, that her Well-beloved is everywhere and in everything, and that everything is He, so that she can distinguish nothing from Him who is in all places without being enclosed in any.

Verse 3. The watchmen that go about the city found me, to whom I said, Saw ye Him whom my soul loveth?

Since I have not found my Beloved in any mortal creature, I have sought Him among those happy spirits *that go about the city* to guard it; *they found me* because they are ever *on the watch,* These are the watchmen whom God has set upon the walls of Jerusalem, and who shall never hold their peace day nor night. *I asked them news of my Well-beloved,* of Him for whom *I burn with love;* but though they themselves possess Him, they could not give Him to me. Methinks I see Mary Magdalene who, not finding Christ in the sepulchre, seeks Him everywhere, asking angels and men, but none can give tidings of the Beloved but Himself.

Verse 4. It was but a little that I passed by them when I found Him whom my soul loveth. I held Him; neither will I let Him go until I bring Him into my mother's house, and into the chamber of her that conceived me.

The soul having thus come forth from self and left all creatures behind, *finds her Well-beloved,* who manifests Himself to her with new charms; which causes her to believe that the blessed moment for the consummation of the divine marriage is at hand, and that she is about to enter into permanent union. She exclaims in a transport of joy, *I have found Him whom my soul loveth,* I embrace Him and will *never let Him go.* For she thinks she can retain Him, and that He only left her on account of some fault she had committed. I will embrace Him so closely, she continues, and will attach myself to Him with so much fidelity, that *I will never let Him go until I have brought Him into my mother's house;* that is, unto the bosom of God, which is *the chamber of her that conceived me,* since He is my source and origin.

But what language is this, O foolish soul? It is His part to take thee there, not thine to lead Him? But love believes everything possible, as Mary was persuaded that she could carry away the body of the Lord. The intense desire which she feels to be there, causes her to forget that she must be there with Him and clothed with Him, and she says she will lead Him there.

Verse 5. I charge you, O ye daughters of Jerusalem, by the roes and the hinds of the fields, that ye stir not up, nor awake my love, till she please.

The Bridegroom, full of compassion, after this first trial of the Spouse (the first deep, interior trial since she rose up to come forth), again communicates his essential union. The poor soul is so carried away with the possession of a treasure which seems to her infinitely greater than before, since it has cost her so dear, that she falls asleep, swoons away, is lost, and seems as if expiring in the arms of love.

We may gather from this that, though the soul suffers greatly in the search after her Beloved, its pain is but a shadow in comparison with the bliss arising from the possession of its adorable object. The same thing is asserted by Saint Paul, who tells us that the greatest sufferings of this life are not worthy to be compared with the glory that shall be revealed in us. Her Well-beloved will not have her waked, because it would hinder her death and retard her happiness.

Verse 6. Who is she that goeth up by the wilderness, like a pillar of smoke, from the incense of myrrh and frankincense and all powders of the perfumer?

The friends of the Bride beholding her adorned with so many perfections, and so filled with grace from the visit of the Bridegroom, testify their astonishment by these expressions: *"Who is she that goeth up by the wilderness, like a pillar of smoke?"*— The Bride becomes so purified in the arms of her Beloved, that she issues from them, like a subtle vapor almost consumed by the fire of love. She is like a smoke that tends directly upward, in consequence of her uprightness and righteousness, and exceedingly subtle, to show that she is already wholly spiritual. This smoke is composed of the choicest odors of all the virtues; but it is worthy of remark, that they are gums that melt and powders that are loose and not solid; solidity and consistence are no longer her part. And whence cometh this upward tending, odoriferous vapor? It cometh from the wilderness of faith. Whither goeth it? To its rest in God.

47

Verse 7. Behold his bed, which is Solomon's; threescore valiant men are about it, of the valiant of Israel.

The Spouse, feeling already quite disengaged from self, thinks that there is but one thing more to be done; and this is true; but alas! what obstacles are yet to be overcome before it is effected. This is to go to God, who is *the bed* of the true *Solomon.* But to reach it, threescore of the valiant men of Israel must be passed through. These valiant warriors are the Divine Attributes who *are about* the royal bed, and prevent the approach of such as are not in a state of perfect annihilation. They are the most valiant in Israel, because it is in these Attributes that Israel, that is, the contemplative soul, finds its strength, and it is also by their means that the power of God is manifested to men.

Verse 8. They all hold swords, being expert in war; every man hath his sword upon his thigh because of fear in the night.

They all hold swords to engage in combat with the soul which, by a secret presumption, attributes to self what belongs to God only; and this causes them to exclaim with united voice; *Who is like unto God?* The Divine Righteousness is the first that comes to fight with and destroy the self-righteousness of the creature, and then comes strength to bring to naught the power of man, and causing him to enter by experience of his own infinite weakness into the strength of the Lord, teaches him to dismiss all thought except of the righteousness of God. His providence assails human foresight; and thus with all the attributes. They are all *armed,* for it is necessary that the soul should be destroyed in these matters before being admitted to the bed of Solomon, becoming a bride and reaching the finishing and consummation of its marriage. These great warriors have *every one his sword upon his thigh.* This sword is nothing else than the word of God, deep, searching and effectual, discovering to the soul its secret presumption, and at the same time destroying it.

This is the uncreated Word, which only manifests itself in the depths of the soul, that it may there operate what it expresses. It is no sooner declared, than, like a stroke of lightning, it reduces to ashes all that opposes it. It operated in the same way when it became incarnate. *For He spake and it was done,* and impressed upon His humanity the characters of His Omnipotence. It entered into the abasement of the creature, to bring down its loftiness, and into its weakness to destroy its strength; it took the form of a sinner that it might annihilate self-righteousness. It does the same in the soul; it abases, weakens and covers it with wretchedness.

But why does the Scripture say that they are thus armed *because of fear in the night?* By this we are to understand, that as self-appropriation is what keeps the soul in darkness, and is the cause of all its melancholy nights, the Divine Attributes are armed against it, that it may not usurp that which belongs only to God.

Verse 9. King Solomon made himself a chariot of the wood of Lebanon.

The Son of God, the King of Glory, *made Himself a chariot* of His Humanity, to which He became united in the Incarnation, intending to be seated upon it to all eternity, and to make of it a triumphal car, upon which He will ride with pomp and splendor in the sight of all His creatures. It is made of the *wood of Lebanon,* because He was descended, according to the flesh, from Patriarchs, Prophets, and Kings, eminent for their sanctity and character. The Word of God is thus in man, as upon the throne of His Majesty, as St. Paul declares that God was in Christ reconciling the world unto Himself.

Christ constructs for Himself in every soul a throne, which He adorns with great magnificence, to become the place of His abode, as well as of His repose and eternal delights; after having bought it with His blood and sanctified it by His grace, that He may reign there as a Sovereign. For as God reigns in Jesus Christ, in the same way Christ reigns in pure hearts, where He finds nothing that either resists or is offensive to Him. This is appointing us a kingdom and making us partakers of His royal state, as His Father had appointed Him a kingdom and shared His glory with Him.

This throne of the King of Kings, then, is made of the wood of Lebanon. The foundation of the spiritual building is the natural ground of man, which is not inaptly represented by the height and value of the trees of Lebanon, inasmuch as it is derived from God Himself, and is made in His image and likeness.

The Spouse of this Canticle is set forth as a model of this august throne, to every other spouse of the Celestial Bridegroom, that they may be animated in the pursuit of a similar felicity. She herself describes the throne, having received new light to scan it with more penetration, in the essential though transitory union, with which she has been just favored. Hence she adds,

Verse 10. He made the pillars thereof of silver, the couch of gold, the ascent thereto of purple; and the midst thereof he strewed with love for the daughters of Jerusalem.

The pillars of the holy Humanity of Jesus Christ are *of silver;* His soul with its powers and His body with its senses being of a finished purity well set forth by the most refined and brilliant silver. *His couch,* which is the Divinity itself, in which Christ subsists in the person of the Word, is clearly expressed by the couch of this mysterious chariot being made *all of gold,* which is often put in the Scriptures for God. *The ascent thereto is adorned with purple,* whereby it is signified, that although the bosom of God the Father, which is the dwelling place of the Word, was His by right of His eternal generation, and though He could have no other, even after becoming man by the decree of the Divine Righteousness, to which He voluntarily submitted; still He could not reascend to His Father, to enter into the fulness of His glory, except by the purple of His blood. *Ought not Christ to have suffered these things and to enter into His glory! The midst* of this triumphal car is adorned with ornaments of great value, well signified by *love* as being the greatest and most precious of all. For is it not Jesus Christ that contains all the treasures of wisdom and knowledge and the fulness of the Godhead bodily? The Holy Spirit was not given by measure to Him. The Holy Spirit, then, fills the midst of this majestic throne; since He is the

Love of the Father and of the Son, and thus the love with which God loves men; and as He is the union of the Divine Persons, so He is the link that binds pure souls to Christ. The Divine Solomon has made all this *for the daughters of Jerusalem,* who are His elect, for whom He has done and suffered all.

In the sanctuary which God prepares for Himself in His beloved, there are, in the same way, *pillars of silver,* which are the gifts of the Holy Spirit, founded upon Divine Grace, which is like pure and shining silver, serving them for material and foundation. *The couch of it is of gold;* for a soul that is fit to serve as a throne and royal couch for Christ should have no other foundation than God Himself, and must be devoid of every created support. *Its ascent thereto is of purple;* for if it is only through much tribulation that we can enter into the kingdom of God and if we must suffer with Christ, in order to reign with Him, in a much higher degree must this be true of those who are called to the first places in the interior kingdom, and who are to be honored in this life with the nuptials of the heavenly Bridegroom, than it is of the ordinary sort of Christians who leave the world, in a salvable state truly, but loaded with debts and imperfections. The amount of crosses, reproaches and destructions suffered by such souls is inconceivable. And lastly, *the midst thereof is strewed with love,* since these living thrones of the Most High being full of love, are also adorned with all the fruits and ornaments of love, such as good works, merits, the fruits of the Spirit, and the practice of the purest and most solid virtues.

Behold your calling, O ye *daughters of Jerusalem!* interior Brides, devoted souls! Behold what the King of Kings, the King of Peace has merited for you and offers to bestow upon you, if you will give Him your love! It is upon this precious foundation that the Bridegroom and the Bride rest the magnificent praises which they mutually interchange in the succeeding chapters.

Verse 11. Go forth, O ye daughters of Zion, and behold King Solomon with the crown wherewith his mother crowned him in the day of his espousals, and in the day of the gladness of his heart.

Christ invites all interior souls, who are *the daughters of Zion, to go forth* out of themselves and their imperfections to *behold King Solomon with the crown* of Glory Bestowed upon Him by God Himself. The Divine Nature is in the light of a *mother* to the human, crowns it, and is at the same time its *diadem.* It crowns Christ *in the day of His espousals* with a glory as sublime as it is infinite and unfading. But what is the Lamb's espousal day? It is the day on which He ascended up into Heaven, where He was received at the right hand of the Father, *a day of* eternal *gladness of heart. Behold, Him,* daughters of Zion! arrayed in all His divine conquests; for He desires to share them with you.

Madame Guyon

CHAPTER 4

VERSE 1. How beautiful thou art, my love; how beautiful thou art! Thou hast doves' eyes, besides what is hid within; thy hair is as a flock of goats that appear from Mount Gilead.

THOUGH THE BRIDEGROOM cannot yet admit the Spouse to His nuptial bed, which is the bosom of His Father, He nevertheless finds her *very fair,* yea, *fairer* than ever. For her faults are no longer flagrant sins, nor scarcely offences; but rather defects in her still hard and contracted nature, which suffers incredible pain in being so enlarged that it may be lost in God. She is then very fair both within and without, and fairer than ever, though she cannot be convinced of it by reason of her recent repulse from being received into God. Hence the Bridegroom assures her that she *is very fair, even without that which is concealed from herself,* and which is more beautiful than anything that appears externally, or that can be expressed or imagined.

Thine eyes, by thy fidelity and simplicity, are like *those of doves.* This quality is both exterior and interior.

The virtue of Simplicity, so highly recommended in the scriptures, causes us to act in respect to God unceasingly, without hesitation; straightforward, without reflections; and supremely, without manifold intentions, motives or designs, with a single eye to the good pleasure of God. When simplicity is perfect, we even commonly act without a thought of it. To act in simplicity with the neighbor, is to act with frankness, without affectation; with sincerity, without disguise, and with liberty, without constraint. These are the eyes and heart of the dove that are dear to Christ.

Thy hair, which represents the affection which springs from thy heart, and which is its ornament, is so separated from earthly things, that it is raised above the most excellent gifts until it arrives at Me. It resembles, in this respect, *the goats* that appear upon the most inaccessible mountains.

Verse 2. Thy teeth are like a flock of sheep that are even shorn, which came up from the washing; whereof every one bears twins, and none is barren among them.

The *teeth* represent the understanding and memory, which serve to chew and masticate the things we desire to know. These powers have been already *purified* as well as the imagination and the fancy, so that there is no longer any confusion; they are appropriately compared to *sheep even shorn,* on account of the simplicity they have acquired by their union with the Divine Persons, where they have been

deprived of their excessive inclination and even of
their power to reason and to act in a self-reflective
and disordered manner, as they formerly did. But
though divested of their operations, they are not by
that process rendered barren or unfruitful; on the
contrary, they bear *double fruit,* and that exceedingly
pure and perfect; for the powers are never more
fruitful than when they are lost with reference to the
creature and vanished in God their centre.

Verse 3. Thy lips are as a scarlet fillet; and thy speech is sweet.
Thy cheeks are like a piece of pomegranate, besides that which is
hidden within.

The *lips* represent the will, which is the mouth of
the soul, because it presses and kisses with affection
what it loves. And as the will of this soul loves only its
God, and all its affections are towards Him, the
Bridegroom compares it to *a scarlet fillet,* thus
signifying the affections reunited in a single will,
which is all love and charity; the whole strength of
this will being reunited in its Divine object.

Thy speech, he adds, *is sweet;* because thy heart
has a language that none but I can understand;
because it speaks only to Me. *Thy cheeks are like a
piece of pomegranate,* which has many seeds, all
contained in a single rind; so thy thoughts are, as it
were, reunited in Me alone by thy pure and perfect
love; and all that I have thus described is as nothing
in comparison with what is yet concealed within thy
deepest centre.

Verse 4. Thy neck is like the tower of David, builded with bulwarks; a thousand shields hang upon it, all the armor of mighty men.

The *neck* is the strength of the soul; it is well likened to the tower of David, because all the strength of the soul is in God, who is the house of Jesus Christ and of David. For this great King insists in many places in the Psalms, that God alone is his support, his refuge, his defence, and, above all, his strong tower. The *bulwarks* that surround it are the total abandonment the soul has made of itself to God. Trust, faith and hope have fortified it in its abandonment; the weaker it is in itself, the stronger it is in God. A *thousand shields hang upon it,* to defend it against its innumerable foes, both visible and invisible, *the armor of such mighty men* that it fears no attack so long as it shall thus remain; for up to this point its state is not yet permanently fixed.

Verse 5. Thy two breasts are like two young roes that are twins, which, feed among the lilies.

The Spouse here receives facility in aiding souls, indicated *by her breasts;* but she does not yet receive it in all the fulness which will subsequently be communicated; it is simply implanted in her as a germ of fruitfulness, the abundance of which is denoted by the *young roes that are twins.* They are *twins* because they issue from the same source, even Jesus Christ; *they feed among the lilies,* because they are fed on the pure doctrine of Jesus Christ and under His example.

Verse 6. Until the day break and the shadows flee away, I will get me to the mountain of myrrh, and to the hill of frankincense.

The Bridegroom interrupts His eulogy of His Spouse, to invite her to follow Him towards the mountain upon which grows myrrh, and to the hills where frankincense was collected. *Until,* says He, *the day* of the new life thou art to receive in My Father, *begin to appear, and the shadows* which envelop thee in the obscurity of the most naked faith, *flee away and vanish, I will get me to the mountain of myrrh;* for thou wilt no longer find me except in bitterness and the cross. It will be, nevertheless, a mountain of exceeding sweet savor to me, for the perfume of thy sufferings will rise towards me as incense, and by their means I shall be enabled to enter into rest within thee.

Verse 7. Thou art all fair, my love, there is no spot in thee.

Until the soul was wholly immersed in bitterness and crosses, though still fair, she was not *all fair;* but now that she is prostrate under the load of trouble and affliction, she is *all fair, and there is no spot* or deformity in her.

She would now be ready for permanent union, if there were not still within her remains of her former harsh, unyielding, bounded and limited nature, which stands in the way of her happiness. It is not a fault in her nor is it even offensive in the sight of God; it is simply a natural defect, derived from Adam, which her Bridegroom will insensibly take away. But, as for herself, though the cross has entirely destroyed her beauty in the eyes of men, in those of her Bridegroom she is *all fair,* and since she has no longer any comeliness of her own, she has become possessed of the true beauty.

Verse 8. Come from Lebanon, my Spouse, come from Lebanon, come; Thou shalt be crowned from the top of Amana, from the peak of Shenir and Hermon, from the dens of the lions, from the mountains of the leopards.

The Bridegroom here calls her by the name of *Spouse,* and invites her to hasten in permitting herself to be destroyed and annihilated, and receive the spiritual marriage. He calls her to her wedding and coronation.

But O Bridegroom! shall I say it? Why so earnestly and so continually invite a spouse to a consummation she so passionately desires? Thou callest her *from Lebanon* though she is in Jerusalem. Is this because Thou sometimes givest the name of Lebanon to Jerusalem, or wouldst Thou, perchance, by the loftiness of this great mountain, indicate the elevation of the Spouse in thine eyes? She has scarce a step to take before she is united to Thee by an everlasting tie, and when she seems to be approaching Thy bed she is repulsed by sixty strong men. Is there not Cruelty in thus powerfully, though sweetly attracting her towards a treasure which she esteems more highly than a thousand lives, and when she seems on the point of obtaining it, roughly repulsing her? O God! Thou invitest, Thou callest, Thou givest the fitness for the state before conferring the state itself, as we give a slight taste of a delicious drink that we may excite a desire for more. Ah! what suffering dost Thou not inflict upon this soul by the delay of that gift which Thou hast promised her?

Come, My Spouse, He says, for there is but a single step to take before thou wilt be so in reality. Until now, I have called thee *My fair one, My Well-beloved, My dove,* but never as yet *My Spouse.* Oh! how sweet is this name! but the reality will be far more pleasant and delightful! *Come,* He pursues, *from the tops of the highest mountains,* that is to say, from the purest practice of the most eminent virtues designated by the mountains of *Amana, Shenir* and *Herman,* which are near Mount Lebanon. However exalted all this may seem to thee, and however high it may in fact be, thou must come up still higher and overtop everything, that thou mayest enter with Me into the bosom of My Father and there rest, without intermediate and by the loss of every means; for immediate and central union can only be accomplished by ascending far above every created thing. But come also *from the lions' dens, and from the mountains of the leopards;* for thou canst arrive at a state so divine only by coming through the most cruel persecutions of men and of devils who are like so many wild beasts. It is now time to rise more than ever above all this, since thou art prepared to be *crowned* as my Bride.

Verse 9. Thou hast wounded my heart, my sister Spouse; thou hast wounded my heart with one of thine eyes and with one tress of thy neck.

Thou art My sister, since we belong to the same Father; My *Spouse,* since I have already betrothed, thee, and there wants but little before our marriage shall be consummated. *My sister, My Spouse!* O words of sweetness to a soul in affliction, whose grief overflows because the beauty she adores and by whom she is so tenderly loved, cannot yet be possessed! *Thou hast wounded My heart!* He says, *thou hast wounded My heart!* Thou hast inflicted, O Spouse, a double wound; one, *by one of thine eyes,* as if He would say, that which has wounded and delighted me to thee, is that all thine afflictions, all thine abasements and thy most extreme deprivations have not caused thee to turn thine eye away from Me that thou mightest behold thyself. Thou hast taken no more notice of the wounds I have caused thee to receive, nor even of those which I myself inflicted, than if they had not been; because thy pure and upright love kept thee so steadily regarding Myself, that it did not permit thee to consider thyself nor thine own interest, but solely to contemplate Me with love as thy sovereign object.

But alas! exclaims this afflicted soul, how is it that I have steadfastly regarded Thee when I do not even know where Thou art? She knows not that her look has become so purified, that being ever direct and unreflective, it escapes her notice and does not perceive that she always sees. And besides, when we can see Him no longer, and have forgotten self and every creature, we must of necessity behold God, and the interior eye is fixed upon Him alone.

The other wound thou hast inflicted upon me, continues the Bridegroom, is by *one tress of thy neck;* by which is plainly meant that every affection of the Bride is concentred in God alone, and that she has lost all her will in His. Thus the abandonment of her entire self to the will of God, by the loss of all separate will, and the integrity with which she clings to God, without any further self-reflections, are the two arrows which have *pierced the heart* of the Bridegroom.

Verse 10. How fair are thy breasts, my sister Spouse! thy breasts are fairer than wine! and the smell of thine ointments than all spices.

The Bridegroom foreseeing all the triumphs that the Bride will accomplish for Him, and how abundant will be the supply of milk from her bosom for the nourishment of innumerable souls, is in an ecstasy of admiration. For it is to be observed, that the further the Spouse advances, the fuller become her breasts, the Bridegroom continually replenishing them for her; whereupon He cries out: *How fair are thy breasts, My sister, My Spouse!* They are more beauteous than wine; for they furnish both wine and milk, one for strong men and the other for babes.

The smell of thine ointments, by which thou drawest souls to Me, *infinitely surpasses all spices.* There will be in thee an odor that none will recognize except those that be far advanced, but which will then attract such and cause them to run after thee, that they may come to Me, and they shall be brought to Me by thee. This secret perfume will astonish those who are ignorant of this mystery. Nevertheless, their experience will compel them to acknowledge thus; I know not what it is of thee that attracts me; it is an admirable perfume which I cannot resist, and yet I cannot divine what it is. This must be the Unction of the Holy Spirit, which the Lord's Christ alone can communicate to the Bride.

Verse 11. Thy lips, O my Spouse, drop as the honeycomb; honey and milk are under thy tongue; and the smell of thy garments is like the smell of Lebanon.

The moment the soul has reached the blessedness of being forever received into her God, she becomes a nursing mother. Fertility is bestowed upon her; she is admitted into the state of the Apostolic life, and from thenceforward *her lips continually drop as the honeycomb,* for the entertainment of souls. It is only her lips and not her words, for it is the Bridegroom who speaks through His Bride, her lips being allowed Him as the means of uttering the Divine Word. *Honey and milk are under the tongue* which I have given thee; it is I that place the honey and the milk there, and that cause them to be dispensed for the good of souls according to their need. The Bride is all honey to those who are to be gained by the sweetness of consolations; she is all milk to such souls as have become perfectly simple and childlike. *The smell of thy* virtues and of the good works with which thou art clothed as *with a garment,* and which are of no account in thy sight, because they are no longer of thyself, is diffused abroad like a sweet smelling perfume.

Verse 12. A garden enclosed is my sister Spouse; a garden enclosed, a fountain sealed.

The holy Bridegroom becomes the eulogist of the Bride, for other purpose than that He may manifest to us what He desires we should become in following her example. *A garden enclosed is My sister, My Spouse,* He declares, *shut up* without and within. For as there is nothing within her which is not absolutely Mine, neither is there anything without, nor in any of her actions, which is not wholly for Me; she is mistress, neither of any of her actions nor of any other thing whatsoever; *she is shut up on every side;* there is no longer anything in her for herself nor for any other creature. She is also a fountain, since she is intimately united to Me, who am the spring whence she derives water to replenish the earth; but I keep her *sealed,* so that not a drop shall escape without My direction, and thus the water that issues thence will be perfectly pure and without the least mixture, as they issue from Myself.

Verse 13. Thy plants are a paradise of pomegranates, with the fruits of the orchard; cypress with spikenard.

Thy fertility shall be so enlarged that it shall be like *a paradise of pomegranates with pleasant fruits.* Union to the source of all, rendering thee useful to all, the Spirit of God will reveal Himself by thee in various places, as we see the pomegranate (which represents souls in the union of love) distributes its sap to every seed that it contains. It is true that the principal sense of this passage concerns the church; but no one would believe the wonderful fruits that a soul thoroughly annihilated would produce in behalf of men, as soon as it was applied to help them. There are fruits of all sorts in this garden, every soul, in addition to the qualities common to all, possessing peculiarities of its own. Thus, one excels in charity, the pomegranate; another in meekness, the apple; another is distinguished by suffering and the odor of its good example, the cypress; another distils devotion, recollection and peace, the spikenard; all are assisted by the annihilated Spouse according to their necessities.

Verse 14. Spikenard and saffron; calamus and cinnamon with all the trees of Lebanon; myrrh and aloes with all the chief ointments.

He here continues the description of the souls, of whom, as the pure result of His goodness, He has made His Spouse the mother; and while He is rehearsing the good qualities of others, He causes them all to be perceived at the same time in her as the channel by which they are distributed.

Verse 15. A fountain of gardens, a well of Living waters, and streams flowing strongly from Lebanon.

This *fountain of gardens* is the Bridegroom Himself, who is the source of the graces which cause spiritual plants to spring up, flourish, grow and bring forth fruit. The Spouse is like *a well of living waters,* and these waters descend from the Bridegroom through the Bride, streaming impetuously from the heights of the Divinity, represented by Mount Lebanon, to overflow the whole earth, that is, all those souls who are sincerely desirous of entering into the interior kingdom, and are willing to endure its toils in the hope of enjoying its fruits.

Verse 16. Arise, O north wind, and come thou south; blow through my garden, and let its spices flow out.

The Bride invites the *Holy Spirit,* the Spirit of life, to come and breathe through her, in order that this garden, thus filled with flowers and fruits, may put forth its spicy perfumes for the help of souls. The Bridegroom, too, requires that the resurrection of his Spouse may be hastened, and that she may receive new life by the in-breathing of that life-giving Spirit, who will reanimate this annihilated soul, to the end that the marriage may be perfectly consummated.

CHAPTER 5

Verse 1. Let my beloved come into his garden and eat the fruit of his appletrees. I am come into my garden, my sister Spouse; I have gathered my myrrh with my spices; I have eaten my honeycomb with my honey; I have drunk my wine with my milk; eat, O friends, drink and be drunken, O dearly be-loved.

THE SPOUSE, who, as her Well-beloved has declared, is a beautiful garden always full of flowers and fruits, earnestly begs Him to come there to enjoy its delights and *to eat His pleasant fruits.* It is as though she were to say, I desire neither beauty nor fertility except for Thee; come, then, *into Thy garden* and possess all things, partake of and use them for the advantage of favored souls, otherwise I deserve them not.—The Well-beloved consents to the desire of the Spouse; He desires indeed to come and partake of everything, but He would have the Bride present to see that He Himself first eats from the table He spreads for His friends. *I have gathered,* He says, *My myrrh;* but it is for thee, My Spouse, for it is thy sustenance, which is nothing but bitterness; for suffering never ceases in this mortal life. Nevertheless, this myrrh is never alone, but is always accompanied by very pleasant spices.—The perfume is for the Bridegroom; the bitter myrrh for the Spouse. As for me, says the Bridegroom, *I have eaten My sweets,* I have *drunk wine and milk,* I have fed upon the sweets of thy love. Enchanted with the generosity of His Bride, He invites all his friends and His children to come and satisfy their hunger and quench their thirst beside His Bride, who is a garden laden with fruits and watered with milk and honey. A soul of this strength has abundant supply for the spiritual needs of all sorts of persons, and can bestow excellent advice upon all who apply to her.

This is also true of the church which invites Christ to come and eat of the fruit of her appletrees, which is simply to collect the fruit of His merits by the sanctification of His predestinated, as He will do it at His second coming. The Bridegroom replies to His beloved Spouse, that *He did come into his garden* when He became incarnate; that He gathered his myrrh with his spices when He suffered the bitterness of His passion, which was accompanied by infinite merits, and sent a perfume up to God the Father. *I have eaten My honeycomb,* He adds, *with My honey.* This is to be understood of his actions and teaching; for He practised what He preached, and ordained nothing for us which He did not first Himself put in action, meriting for us, by the very things which He practised, the grace for what He requires of us. Thus the life of Christ was like a honeycomb, the divine order and sweetness of which constituted His meat and drink, and His happiness, in the view of the glory which His Father would receive from it, and the advantage it would be to men. *I have*

drunk My wine with My milk. What wine is this, O
Saviour divine, which Thou hast drunk and with
which Thou wert so deeply intoxicated as to entirely
forget Thyself? It was the overpowering love He bore
to men which caused Him to forget that He was God,
and think only on their salvation. He was so
intoxicated with it, that it is said of Him by a Prophet,
that He should be loaded with reproaches, such was
the strength of His love. *He drank wine with His milk,*
when He drank His own blood in the supper, which,
under the semblance of wine, was virgin milk. The
milk, again, was the influx of the Divinity of Christ
into His humanity.

This Divine Saviour invites thither all His elect,
who desire to be nourished like Him upon suffering,
reproaches and ignominy, on the love of His example
and His pure doctrine, which will be delicious *wine
and milk* for them; wine, which shall give them
strength and courage to perform every thing
required of them, and milk, which shall delight them
by the sweetness of the doctrine that shall be taught
them.

We are, then, all invited to hear and imitate Jesus
Christ.

Verse 2. I sleep, but my heart waketh; it is the voice of my
beloved that knocketh, saying, Open to me, my sister, my love, my
dove, my undefiled; for my head is filled with dew, and my locks
with the drops of the night.

The soul that watches for its God, experiences
that, although its exterior appears dead, and, as it
were, stunned and benumbed, like a body in a deep
sleep, still the heart constantly retains a secret and

hidden vigor, which preserves it in union with God. Those souls which are far advanced, frequently experience, in addition, a very surprising thing, that often, during the night, they are but half asleep, as it were, and that God seems to operate more powerfully in them in the night and during sleep, than during the day.

While thus asleep, the soul hears clearly the voice of the Well-beloved, who knocks at the door. He desires to make Himself heard; He says, *Open to Me, My sister;* I am come to thee, *My love,* whom I have chosen above all others to be My Bride; *My dove* in simplicity, My perfect one, My beautiful, *My undefiled.* Reflect that *My head is fitted* with what I have suffered for thee during the darkness of My mortal life, and that for thy sake I have been saturated with *the drops of the night* of the most cruel persecutions. I come now to thee, to make thee partaker of My reproaches, My ignominy, and My confusion. Thou hast, hitherto, tasted but the bitterness of the cross, thou hast not yet experienced its ignominy and confusion. One is quite different from the other, as thou art about to learn from, a terrible experience.

Verse 3. I have put off my coat; how shall I put it on? I have washed my feet; how shall I defile them?

The Spouse perceiving the intention of the Bridegroom to make her a partaker of His ignominy, is sadly fearful; and is now as much dejected at her threatened disgrace as she was before bold and courageous in accepting the cross. There are many who are content to bear the cross; but there is scarcely a single one that is willing to bear its infamy.

The soul is apprehensive of two things, when her possible ignominy is presented; one, that she may be reinvested with what she has lately thrown aside, to wit, self and her natural defects; the other, lest she should become defiled in the affections of the creature. *I have put off my coat,* says she, self, my faults, and all the residue of the old Adam that was in me; *how can I put it on again?* And yet I cannot conceive of anything else that can cause my humiliation and confusion; for as to the contempt put upon me by the creature, without my having caused it by my own fault, it is a pleasure and a glory to me, trusting that it will glorify my God and render me more acceptable in His sight. *I have washed* and purifed my affections, so that there is nothing in me that is not wholly devoted to my Well-beloved, *how shall I again defile them* by commerce with the creature?

Ah, poor blinded one! what wouldst thou ward off? The Bridegroom only desired to try thy fidelity and see if thou wert in truth ready to do all His will. He was despised and rejected of men, esteemed stricken, smitten of God and afflicted, and was numbered with the transgressors, He who was innocence itself; and thou, who art so loaded with guilt, yet canst not bear to be reproached with it! Ah! wilt thou not suffer severely for thy resistance?

Verse 4. My beloved put in his hand through the opening, and my bowels thrilled at his touch.

The Well-beloved, notwithstanding the resistance of his Bride, *puts in his hand* by a little opening which yet remains to Him, that is, a remnant of abandonment, in spite of the repugnance of the soul to abandon herself so absolutely. A soul in this degree has a depth of submission to every will of God that will refuse him nothing; but when he unfolds his plans in detail, and using the rights He has acquired over her, calls for the last renunciation and the extremest sacrifices, then it is that *all her bowels thrill at His touch;* and she finds trouble where she anticipated none. This difficulty arises from the fact that she was attached to something, without being aware of it. All her nature is in a tremor at this touch, for it is painful, and causes the most exquisite anguish to the soul, as was experienced by the most patient of men, when, after having suffered the most inconceivable ills without complaint, he could not refrain from crying out when the finger of God was laid upon him, *Have pity upon me, have pity upon me, O ye my friends; for the hand of God hath touched me.* Thus the Spouse trembles at the touch of God.

How jealous art Thou, O Divine Spouse, that Thy bride should do all Thy will, since a simple excuse that seemed so just offends Thee so deeply! Couldst Thou not have hindered so dear and so faithful a Spouse from offering this resistance? But it was necessary for her perfection. The Bridegroom permits the presence of the fault, that He may punish, and at the same time purge her from that complacency in her own purity and innocence which still remained, and from the repugnance which she felt at being stripped of her own righteousness; for though she knew perfectly well that her righteousness belonged to the Bride-groom, she was still somewhat attached to it, and appropriated some of the credit of it to herself.

Verse 5. I rose up to open to my beloved; my hands dropped with myrrh, and my fingers were bathed with the choicest myrrh.

No sooner does the soul perceive her fault than she hastens to repent, and to *rise up,* by a renewal of her abandonment and an extension of her sacrifice. It is not done, however, without pain and bitterness; the inferior part and the whole of nature are seized with sadness and affright; all her actions even, are rendered more painful and bitter; but the bitterness is far beyond anything she has yet experienced.

Verse 6. I withdrew the bolt of my door for my Beloved; but he had turned aside and was gone. My soul melted when he spake; I sought him, and found him not; I called him, but he gave me no answer.

This is as though the soul were to say, I have removed the barrier which hindered my total loss and the consummation of my marriage; for that can only take place after total loss. I have therefore removed this barrier by the most courageous abandonment and the purest sacrifice that ever was beheld.—*I have opened to my Beloved,* thinking that He would come in and heal the grief He had caused by His touch; but alas! the blow would be too mild if the remedy were so promptly applied! He hides, He flies, *He is turned aside, and is gone;* He leaves to His afflicted Spouse nothing but the wound He had inflicted, the pain of her fault, and the impurity she conceives herself to have contracted in rising.

The goodness of the Bridegroom, nevertheless, is so great, that, though He hides Himself, He does not cease to bestow great favors upon His friends; and the greater, as the privations are longer and more severe. Thus did He to His Spouse, who was now in a new and most favorable state of mind, though she knew it not. *Her soul melted when He spake,* and by this softening she lost those hard and unyielding characteristics that prevented the consummation of the spiritual marriage, so that she is now wholly prepared to flow sweetly into her Original. *I sought Him, but I found Him not; I called Him, but He gave me no answer!* O inconceivable affliction!

Verse 7. The watchmen that went about the city found me; they smote me, they wounded me; the keepers of the walls took away my veil from me.

Poor, suffering Spouse! never has anything like this occurred before; for hitherto the Bridegroom kept thee; thou hast securely dwelt under His shadow; thou wert in assurance in His arms; but since he has departed by thy fault, ah! what has happened! Thou thoughtedst thou hadst already suffered much by the numerous trials to which He had subjected thy fidelity; but they were a small matter in comparison with what remains to be suffered. What thou hast suffered with Him was but the shadow of suffering, and thou hadst no reason to expect any less. Thinkest thou to espouse a God, covered with wounds, torn with nails and despoiled of everything, without being treated in the same manner? The soul finds herself *smitten and wounded of them that kept the walls of the city;* they who had not hitherto dared to attack her, and who nevertheless incessantly watched her, now take their time to smite her. Who are these watchmen? They are the ministers of God's justice; they wound her and take away that covering so dear to her, the veil of her own righteousness.

Ah, miserable Spouse! what wilt thou now do in thy pitiable state? The Bridegroom will have nothing more to do with thee after so sad an accident, which has subjected thee to the humiliation of being maltreated by soldiers, of being wounded by them, and even of leaving thy veil, thy principal ornament, in their hands! If thou continuest still to seek thy Beloved, thou wilt be called mad to present thyself before Him in such a plight, and still if thou dost not search for Him thou wilt die of longing; thou art truly in a pitiable case!

Verse 8. I charge you, O daughters of Jerusalem, if ye find my beloved, that ye tell him that I am sick of love.

True love has no eyes for self. This poor afflicted Spouse forgets her still bleeding wounds, she forgets her loss, she does not even refer to it; she thinks solely upon Him whom she loves, and she seeks Him with so much the more perseverance as she finds more obstacles in the way. She calls upon enlightened souls and says to them, O ye, to whom my Beloved will no doubt reveal Himself, *I charge you by Himself to tell Him that I am sick of love.* What, O fairest of women, wouldst thou not that we should tell Him of thy wounds, and relate what thou hast undergone in seeking Him? Ah no! answers the generous soul, I am abundantly overpaid for all my sufferings, since I have borne them for Him, and I prefer them to the greatest good; say but one word to my Beloved, *that I am sick of love!* The wound made by His love in the depths of my heart is so acute, that I am insensible to all exterior pains; yea, I can even say, that in comparison they are a delight.

Verse 9. What is thy beloved, more than another beloved, O thou fairest among women! what is thy beloved, more than another beloved, that thou dost so charge us?

The daughters of Jerusalem do not cease to call her the *fairest among women,* because her most painful wounds are hidden, and those which are exposed even add lustre to her beauty. They are astonished at beholding a love so strong, so constant and so faithful in the midst of so many disasters. They inquire, *Who is this Well-beloved?* For, say they, He must be of unequalled attraction, thus to engage His Spouse; for though these souls are spiritual, they are not yet sufficiently advanced to comprehend so straight and naked a path.

Had the bride thought of herself, she would have said, *Call me not fair,* she would have used some words of humility, but she is incapable of that; she has but one thought, the search of her Beloved. She can only speak of Him; she can think of nothing else, and though she should behold herself plunged into an abyss, it would excite no emotion in her. The reasoning she lately indulged in, through fear of becoming defiled, has cost her too dearly, since it has occasioned the absence of the Bridegroom. Instructed thus by her sad experience, she cannot look a moment at herself, and though she were as frightful as she is lovely, she could not think of it.

Verse 10. My beloved is white and ruddy, the chiefest among ten thousand.

My Well-beloved, replies the Spouse, *is white* by His purity, innocence and simplicity. *He is ruddy* by His charity, and because He has chosen to be dyed and purpled in His own blood. He is white by His frankness, ruddy by the fire of His love. He is *chiefest among ten thousand,* that is to say, He is above all I have chosen and preferred Him to every other. His Father has chosen Him above all the children of men as *His Beloved Son in whom He is well pleased.* In short, if you would know, O my young and tender sisters, who it is that I so passionately love, it is He *who is fairer than the children of men, for grace is poured into His lips.* It is He who is *the brightness of everlasting light, the unspotted mirror of the power of God, and the image of His goodness.* Judge ye, if I am not right in bestowing upon Him the whole strength of my love!

Verse 11. His head is as the most fine gold, his locks as the clusters of the palm, black as a raven.

By *the locks* covering his head are to be understood the holy humanity which covers and conceals the Divinity. These same locks, or this humanity extended upon the cross, are like the clusters of the palm; for there, dying for men, He achieved His victory over the enemies and obtained for them the fruits of His redemption, which had been promised us through His death. Then the bud of the palm-tree opened and the church emerged from the heart of her Bridegroom. There the adorable humanity appeared *black as a raven,* for it was not only covered with wounds, but also loaded with the sins and blackness of all men, and this, although it was in truth unparalleled in whiteness and purity. There Christ appeared *a worm, and no man; a reproach of men, and despised of the people.* Was He not black? and yet this blackness only set off His beauty, for it was only laid upon Him that it might be taken off from the whole world.

Verse 12. His eyes are like a dove's by the rivers of waters, washed with milk, and sitting beside overflowing streams.

She goes on holding up to admiration the perfection of her Bridegroom; His abundance and His wonderful qualities are the joy of the Spouse, in the midst of her misery. *His eyes,* says she, are so pure, so chaste and so simple, His knowledge so purified from everything material, that *they are like dove's;* not like doves of any common beauty, but doves washed in the milk of divine grace, which, having been given to Him without measure, has filled Him *with all the treasures of the wisdom and knowledge of God.* He is beside *the small streams* in lowly souls, who, even though but little advanced, are not the less agreeable to Him, by reason of their lowliness; especially when they have learned to make use of it. But He makes His constant abode in abandoned souls, near those *rapid and overflowing streams* that are arrested by nothing in their course, and that swell and rush on with the greater impetuosity when any obstacle seeks to detain them.

Verse 13. His cheeks are as a bed of spices, prepared by the perfumers; His lips like lilies, dropping choice myrrh.

The cheeks of the Bridegroom represent the two parts of His soul, the superior and inferior, which are arranged in such an order that nothing can be conceived more admirable, and which give forth an inconceivable perfume. And as the cheeks are joined to the head, so His noble and beauteous soul is joined to His Divinity. *The beds of spices* signify the powers and interior faculties of His holy humanity, which are all perfectly well ordered. It was indeed a skilful perfumer who chose and arranged them, for it was the Holy Spirit that ordered the whole internal and external man Christ Jesus. *His lips* are well compared to *lilies,* but they are the red lilies common in Syria, of exceeding beauty. What lips can be more ruby, or fairer or sweeter than those that dispense the words of spirit and life, and of the knowledge of eternal life? They also distil *an excellent myrrh,* for the teaching of Christ leads to repentance, the mortification of the passions, and continual abandonment.

Verse 14. His hands are turned as of gold, set with hyacinths; his belly is ivory, set with sapphires.

By *His hands* are to be understood His external and internal operations; the interior are *all gold,* for they contemplate nothing less than rendering to God the Father everything received from Him. They are *turned* or *fashioned in the lathe,* to show that He receives nothing from His Father which He does not render to Him again, and that He retains nothing; for He is faithful to give up His kingdom, into the hands of His God and Father. They are *set with hyacinths;* for every one of his interior operations is distinguished by the most eminent degree of that virtue to which they belong, especially of devotion to His Father and mercy toward man. His exterior operations are dispensing, liberal and open in favor of men. His hands are rounded; they can retain nothing, and they are full of the most excellent grace and mercy, which He unceasingly communicates and distributes to His needy creatures.

His Humanity, represented by *his belly,* is compared to *ivory,* because everything in it is exceedingly pure and solid, since all is united to God and reposes upon the Divinity. It is likewise adorned and embellished with all possible perfections, which shine in it like so many precious stones.

Verse 15. His legs are as pillars of marble, set upon sockets of fine gold; his countenance is as Lebanon, excellent as the cedars.

The whole lower part of the body, here spoken of as *the legs and feet* that sustain it, is taken for the flesh of the Savior, and is well represented by *marble,* by reason of its incorruptibility. For although for a few hours it yielded to death, yet being *set upon a socket of fine gold,* that is, united to the Divinity, it did not see corruption, and that noble building of God, sustained by the Word of God, to which it owes its incorruptibility, will never be dissolved. *His countenance* is beautiful *even as Lebanon,* which is of vast extent and exceedingly fertile, for there are planted the cedars, that is, the saints. But though all the saints are planted in Jesus Christ, He is nevertheless elect, like them, as regards His humanity, being the first fruits of them that are saved; and He is elected for all men, for there is none elected that is not chosen in Him and by Him; it is He that has merited their election, all having been predestinated to be conformed to the glory of Christ, that He might be the first born among many brethren.

Verse 16. His throat is most sweet, yea, he is altogether lovely. This is my beloved, and this is my Friend, O daughters of Jerusalem.

The good qualities of ordinary things may be sufficiently well expressed by ordinary phrases of commendation, but there are some subjects so above expression that they can only be worthily admired by declaring them above all praise. Such is the Divine Bridegroom, who, by the excess of His perfections, renders His Bride dumb when she endeavors most worthily to praise Him, that all hearts and minds may be attracted to Him. Her passion causes her to burst out into the praise of some of the excellencies which seem to her most comely in the Bridegroom: but as if recovering somewhat from her ecstasy of love, and ashamed of having desired to express what is inexpressible, she condemns herself to sudden silence, thus putting a disordered termination to an address which she uttered as much to find vent for her own passion, as to invite her companions to love Him of whom she is so enamored. Her silence is thus preceded by these few words only, *His throat is most sweet.*

As the throat is the organ of the voice, she thus signifies that He is the expression of the Divinity, and that thus, as God, He is superior to all attributes and qualities. If any are attributed to Him, it is simply an accommodation to the weakness of the creature that knows no other way of expressing itself.—Then giving herself up to transport, she exclaims, *Yea, He is altogether lovely!* As though she would say, O my companions! believe me not because I have told you of my Well-beloved; but judge for yourselves; taste that He is good for yourselves, and then you will understand the force and uprightness of my love. He is to be desired, too, not only because He is the desire of the everlasting hills, and is the desire of all nations, but also because our desire should be to share in His greatness according to our weakness; for He may be imitated by all, though not in all His perfection. This is He, O daughters of Jerusalem, who is possessed of all these rare beauties, and infinitely more than I know how to declare, and whom I love and seek, and of whom I am desperately enamored. Judge if I be not rightly sick of love.

CHAPTER 6

VERSE 1. Whither is thy beloved gone, O thou fairest among women? Whither is thy beloved turned aside? that we may seek him with thee.

THIS soul in its abandonment and grief becomes a great missionary; she preaches the perfections, the sweetness and the infinite loveliness of Him whom she loves, with so much eloquence to her companions, that they are all inspired with a desire to seek Him with her, and to know Him themselves. O conquering Love! when Thou fliest away most rudely, then Thou achievest the most victories! and this soul, impetuous as a torrent by reason of her violent love, carries along with her every one she meets. Ah! who would not desire to see and seek so desirable a lover? O yea who are now uselessly throwing away your affections in the amusements of the world, why not join in this search? How infinitely happy would it make you!

Verse 2. My beloved is gone down into His garden, to the beds of spices, to feed in the gardens and to gather lilies.

O blessed soul! After thy long search, at last thou hast news of thy Beloved! With great confidence thou didst declare that thou wouldst hold Him so firmly that He should never escape, and yet thou hast let Him go farther off than ever! Alas! she says, I was ignorant and rash; I did not reflect that it was not for me to retain Him; that it is His own prerogative to bestow or withdraw Himself, as seems good to Him, and that I ought to will only His will, and to be content with His coming and going. I confess that mine was an interested love, though I knew it not; I preferred my own pleasure in loving, seeing and possessing Him to His good pleasure.—Ah! could I but once behold Him again, I would do so no longer; I would let Him come and go at His own will, and that would be the way to lose Him no more. I know, nevertheless, that He *is gone down into His garden;* my Well-beloved is in my soul, but He is so exclusively there for Himself that I desire no part in it. He is in the most interior centre, in the most sublime part where is found that which is most sweet smelling. There is where God dwells, the source and seat of every virtue; there He comes to feed on what belongs to Him only, for there is nothing there that belongs to me or is for me. He takes His pleasure in the garden which He has planted, cultivated and caused to bear fruit by his life-giving heat. Let Him gather His lilies, then! let all the purity be for Him! let Him have all the pleasure and all the profit from it!

Verse 3. I am my beloved's, and my beloved is mine; He feedeth among the lilies.

86

The moment the soul is wholly freed from self-appropriation, she is all ready to be received into the nuptial couch of the Bridegroom, where she is no sooner introduced, than, tasting the chaste and holy delights of the Kiss of his mouth, which she desired at first, and which she now enjoys in that Essential Union, which has been bestowed upon her, she cannot refrain from expressing her joy in these words, *I am my Beloved's, and my Beloved is mine!* O wonderful gain! I can describe it no farther than that I am unreservedly given up to my Beloved, and that I possess him without obstacle, hindrance or restraint!

O, worthy to be envied of the angels! Thou hast at last discovered thy Well-beloved; and though thou art no longer so bold as to say that thou wilt never let Him go, thou hast Him more securely than ever. Thou wilt never lose Him more! Who would not rejoice with thee on so joyful an occasion!—Thou art so fully thy Beloved's that nothing hinders thee from being lost in Him; since thou has been wholly melted by the heat of his love, thou hast been ready to be poured into Him as into thy final end. Ah! exclaims this imcomparable Spouse, if I am wholly His, He also is wholly mine! for I experience anew of His goodness; He bestows Himself upon me in a manner as unspeakable as it is new; He compensates my pains with the tenderest caresses; He feeds among the lilies of my purity; those of the soul, far more precious to Him than those of the flesh, are an absolute freedom from self-appropriation; a soul freed from self is a virgin soul; those of the body are the integrity of the senses.

Verse 4. Thou art beautiful, O my love, sweet and comely as
Jerusalem, terrible as an army set in array.

The Bridegroom finding His bride entirely free
from self, dissolved and prepared for the
consummation of the marriage, and to be received
into a state of permanent and lasting union with
Himself, admires her beauty; He tells her that she *is
beautiful* because He finds in her a certain charm and
sweetness which approaches the divine. *Thou art
comely,* He continues, *as Jerusalem;* for since thou
hast lost everything of thine own to devote it wholly
to Me, thou art adorned and embellished with all that
is Mine, and art joint possessor of all my inheritance.
I find thee entirely fitted to be My dwelling-place as I
desire to be thine; thou shalt dwell in Me and I in
thee.

But while thou hast so many charms and so
much sweetness for Me, thou art *terrible* to the devil
and to sin *as an army in array;* thou puttest to flight
thine enemies without a blow, for they fear thee as
much as Me, since thou art become one spirit with
God, by the loss of thyself in Me.

Ah! poor souls! ye who are engaged your whole
lifetime in fierce combat and achieve but insignificant
victories, though at the cost of many wounds! if ye
would but earnestly give yourselves up to God and
abandon yourselves to Him, you would be more
formidable and more terrible than an infinite army
drawn up in order of battle!

Verse 4. Turn away thine eyes from me, because they have made
me to flee away; thy hair is as a flock of goats that appear from
Gilead.

It is impossible to conceive the delicacy of the love of God, and the extremity of purity which He requires of souls that are to be His Brides; the perfection of one state is the imperfection of another. Heretofore the Bridegroom rejoiced infinitely that His Spouse never turned her eyes away from Him; now, He desires her not to look at Him; He tells her that *her eyes have made Him to flee away.* When once the soul has begun to flow into her God, as a river into its original source, she must be wholly submerged and lost in Him. She must then lose the perceptible vision of God and every distinct knowledge, however ever small it may be; sight and knowledge exist no longer where there is neither division nor distinction, but a perfect fusion. The creature, in this state, cannot look at God without beholding herself, and perceiving at the same time the working of His love. Now, the whole of this must be concealed and hidden away from her sight, that like the Seraphim she may have her eyes veiled, and may never see anything more in this life. That is, she is not to will to see anything or to make any discoveries of herself, which she cannot do without infidelity. But this is no hindrance to God's causing her to discover and understand whatever He pleases. Nothing remains uncovered but the heart, for it is impossible to love too much.

When I speak of distinction, I do not mean the distinction of some divine perfection in God Himself, for that is gone long since; for since the first absorption, the soul has had but a single view of God in her by a confused and general faith, with no distinction of attributes or perfections; and though she has often spoken of the greatness and sovereign qualities of her Well-beloved, it was only done for the purpose of winning souls, and not for any need in herself of these distinct views, which are given her according to necessity, either in speaking or writing. The distinction I now refer to is that between God and the soul. Here the soul cannot and ought not any longer to make such a distinction; God is she and she is God, since by the consummation of the marriage she is absorbed into God and lost in Him, without power to distinguish or find herself again. The true consummation of the marriage causes an admixture of the soul with God so great and so intimate that she can distinguish and see herself no longer, and it is this fusion which diversifies, so to speak, the actions of the creature arrived at this lofty and sublime position; for they emanate from a principle which is wholly divine, in consequence of the unity which has been effected between God and the soul melted and absorbed in Him, God becoming the principle of her actions and words, though they are spoken and manifested externally through her.

The marriage of the body, whereby two persons are rendered one flesh, is but a faint image of this, by which, in the words of St. Paul, God and the soul become one spirit. Many are exceedingly anxious to know when the spiritual marriage takes place; it is easy to ascertain this, from what has been said. The Betrothal, or mutual engagement, is made in the union of the powers when the soul surrenders herself wholly to God, and God gives Himself wholly to the soul, with the intention of admitting her to union; this is an agreement and mutual promise. But ah! what a distance is yet to be travelled, and what sufferings to be undergone before this eagerly desired union can be granted or consummated! The Marriage takes place when the soul falls dead and senseless into the arms of the Bridegroom, who, beholding her more fitted for it, receives her into union. But the Consummation of the marriage does not come to pass until the soul is so melted, annihilated and freed from self, that it can unreservedly flow into God. Then is accomplished that admirable fusion of the creature and the Creator which brings them into unity, so to speak, though with such an infinite disproportion as exists between a single drop of water and the ocean. The drop has become ocean, but it forever remains a little drop, though it has become assimilated in character with the waters of the ocean, and thus fit to be mingled with it and to make but one ocean with it.

If it be said that some saints and some authors have placed the divine marriage in states less advanced than the one that is here described, I reply, that it is because they mistook the *betrothal* for the *marriage* and the *marriage* for the *consummation;* and in speaking with freedom they do not always distinguish exactly these degrees, in the same way that, the very first steps of the interior road are frequently mistaken for Divine Union itself. Every soul that has been admitted to the privilege of betrothal considers herself a Bride; and very naturally, because the Bridegroom so calls her, as we have seen in this very song. Experience and divine illumination alone can enable any one to distinguish the difference.

The Bridegroom again compares the thoughts of His Spouse represented by her *hair* to *goats that appear from Gilead;* not to goats that are standing still, for the mind of such persons is so clear and empty of thoughts, that those which come appear only for a moment, and for just so long a time as is necessary to produce the effect God would work by them.

Verse 5. Thy teeth are as a flock of sheep which go up from the washing, whereof every one beareth twins, and there is not one barren among them.

The Bridegroom repeats to his Bride what He has already once declared, to show her that she has now in full reality what she then had only in the germ. Her *teeth* are her powers, which are now become so innocent, pure and cleansed, that they are perfectly *washed.* The *flocks* which they resemble, are no longer shorn, as they were before, but facility in the use of her powers in an admirable manner, and without confusion, is restored; for the memory now only recalls what the occasion demands, according to the Spirit of God, and without disordered images, and in the right time. They *are not barren,* being endowed with a double fertility; doing more than they have ever accomplished before, and doing it better.

Verse 6. As the rind of a pomegranate are thy cheeks, besides that which is hidden within.

As the rind of the pomegranate is the least part of it, and includes all its excellence, so with this soul, its exterior appears of small account in comparison with *what is concealed within.* The interior is filled with, the purest charity and the most advanced graces, but hidden under a very common exterior; for God takes pleasure in hiding away the souls He destines for Himself. Men are not worthy to know them, though the angels admire and respect them even under the humblest external form in the world. Those who judge by the outward appearance alone would believe them very ordinary persons, though they are the delight of God.

These are not they who astonish the world by miracles, or the possession of extraordinary gifts; these things are a small matter in their eyes. God hides them for Himself, and is so jealous of them that he will not expose them to the eyes of men, but, on the contrary, He seals them with His seal, as He Himself declares that His Bride is a *fountain sealed*, whereof He Himself is the seal. But why does He keep her sealed? Because *love is as strong as death and jealousy as cruel as the grave*. How completely the matter is here expressed, for, as death takes away everything from him whom it holds, so Love snatches everything away from the soul and conceals it in the secret recesses of a living sepulchre. The jealousy of God is as cruel as hell, for it will spare no means whatever to possess itself fully of the Spouse.

I shall be reminded, perhaps, that this soul cannot be so hidden, inasmuch as she is a help to her neighbor. But I reply, that this is the very thing that most subjects her to humiliation, God making use of it to render the soul more contemptible because of the contradictions which she must experience. It is true that those who apply to her and are in a state to receive some communication of the grace which is in her, perceive its effects; but besides that, these souls themselves are exceedingly hidden. God generally permits the humble exterior to the chosen soul to offend even those who are made partakers of her grace, so that they often separate themselves from her after God has produced the effect He intended by her means.

The Bridegroom in this treats the Spouse like Himself.—Were not all those whom he had gained for His Father offended because of Him? Examine for a moment the life of Christ; was there ever anything more ordinary as to the exterior? Those who accomplish more extraordinary things are copies of those saints of whom Christ said that they should do greater works than He did. The souls of whom we now speak are other Christs, which is the reason why we perceive in them less the features of the saints; but if we seek for the marks of the Lord Jesus we shall find them most clearly there. Nevertheless, he is a stumbling-block to the Jews, and to the Greeks foolishness. These souls frequently, in their simplicity, offend those who are rather attached to legal forms than to the simplicity of the Gospel, and regard only the rind of the pomegranate without penetrating any further within.

O ye who are thus misled, remember that the pomegranate, to which the Spouse is so aptly compared, has a rind very contemptible in appearance, notwithstanding it contains the most excellent of fruits and the most agreeable both to the eye and the palate. This is the admirable order of charity which the Bridegroom began to introduce into the heart of His Spouse when He brought her into His store-chambers, and which is here finished, the pomegranate being now fully ripened.

Verse 7. There are threescore queens and fourscore concubines, and virgins without number.

The Bridegroom declares that there are chosen souls like *queens;* others of a lower rank, who participate in his peculiar favors, though they have not the prerogative of sovereigns, and great numbers of souls belonging to Him in the ordinary way and who are beginning to sigh for union with Him; but His Bride surpasses them all in the affection He has for her. O God! to what happiness hast Thou raised Thy Spouse! There are some who appear like queens, elevated above the rest by the splendor of their virtues; there are many others upon whom Thou bestowest Thy caresses, but this Thy Spouse is more to Thee alone than all the others together.

Verse 8. My dove, my undefiled, is but one; she is the only one of her mother; she is the choice one of her that bare her. The daughters saw her and blessed her; yea, the queens and the concubines, and they praised her.

Though the primary sense of this verse refers to the ever-blessed Mary and the universal Church, still, as there is nothing attributed to the church as a mystical body, which is not proportionately true of souls as its members, especially when they are perfectly pure; so it may be said that there are souls in every age whom God has elected in a very peculiar manner. He here declares, then, that this soul, in whom the marriage has been consummated by her total annihilation and absolute loss, is a *dove* in simplicity, and *but one,* for there are few that resemble her; she is also *but one,* for she is restored in God to the perfect unity of her origin. She is perfect, but with the perfection of God, and because she is freed from self and disengaged from her hard, cramped and limited nature, from the time that by her entire renunciation she entered into the innocence of God. She is perfect in her interior, by the loss of all self-seeking whatever.

It is to be remarked here, that whatever praises the Bridegroom may have hitherto bestowed upon the Spouse, He has never called her *one* and *perfect* until she had entirely sunk into His Divine Unity; for these qualities are only to be found in God when the soul is perfected in Him in, a permanent and enduring state.

She is the *only one of her mother,* because she has lost all the multiplicity of nature and become separate from everything that is natural. She is the choice one of that wisdom that bare her in order that she might be lost in His bosom.

The most interior souls have beheld her; for God ordinarily permits such souls to be a little known, sometimes bestowing some discernment of their state upon other deeply spiritual souls, who are delighted with the sight, and, admiring their perfection, pronounce them *blessed.* The queens, who are souls high in the esteem of every one, and also those other common souls inferior in merit, contribute also great praises, because they feel the effect of the grace communicated to them.

Though this may seem to contradict what has been said a little way back, there is, in fact, no inconsistency; what is here said to be understood of the Apostolic state of Christ which He received both as King and Savior, on the very spot where a little while after He was executed as a felon.

Verse 9. Who is she that cometh forth as the rising morning, fair as the moon, clear as the sun, and terrible as an army in battle-array.

A chorus of the companions of the Bridegroom are here admiring the beauty of His Bride. *Who is she,* say they, *that cometh forth,* rising gradually? For it must be understood that the soul, though in union with God, is raised by degrees, and perfected in this divine life until she arrives in the eternal mansions. She rises in God imperceptibly, like the day breaking, until she comes to the perfect day and brightness of noon, which is the glory of Heaven. But this everlasting day has its beginning in this life. *She is fair as the moon,* for she derives all her beauty from the sun. *She is clear as the sun,* because she is in union with Christ, being a partaker of His glory and lost with Him in God. But she is terrible and fearful to devils, to sin, to the world, and to self-love, as an army drawn up in order of battle and ready for the fight.

Verse 10. I went down into the garden of nuts to see the fruits of the valley, and to see whether the vine flourished and the pomegranates budded.

The soul is not yet so firmly established in God that she cannot still cast some looks upon self; it is an unfaithfulness, but it is rare and only arises from weakness. The Bridegroom has permitted His bride to commit this slight fault, to show us how much injury is caused by self reflection in the most advanced states. She entered for a moment again into self under the most specious pretexts in the world, to behold the fruits of her annihilation, to see if *the vine flourished,* if she were advancing, if her charity were fruitful. Does not that appear very natural, right and reasonable?

Verse 11. I knew nothing; my soul troubled me on account of the chariots of Aminadab.

I did it, she says, without thought, and not intending to do evil nor to displease my Well-beloved, but no sooner was it done than my soul was in trouble because of the chariots of Aminadab; that is, by thousands and thousands of reflections, that revolved in my head like so many disastrous chariots, which would have accomplished my destruction, had not His hand sustained me.

Verse 12. Return, return, O Shulamite! return, return, that we may look upon thee.

The return of the Spouse is as ready and sincere as her fault had been slight and unintentional, wherefore, her companions did not perceive that she had wandered. The only thing that they observed, and at which they were much astonished was, that scarcely had she finished declaring to them the loveliness and beauty of the Bridegroom before she disappeared from their eyes, because she was then at once admitted to the marriage supper of the Lamb. She thus became so elevated above herself and every other creature, that other souls having entirely lost sight of her, beg her to return to them, that they may behold her in her glory and joy as they have seen her in her grief. *Return,* they cry, *O Shulamite!* temple of peace, return to instruct us both by thy example and by thy precept, the way we must take to attain the blessedness that thou possessest; return, that thou mayest be our guide, our support, our consolation; return, that thou mayest take us with thee.

CHAPTER 7

VERSE 1. What will ye see in the Shulamite, but the companies of camps? How beautiful are thy feet with shoes, O prince's daughter! the joints of thy thighs are like jewels; the work of the hands of a cunning workman.

THE Bridegroom replies in place of his Spouse to those who so earnestly insist on her turning towards them, as though not pleased that they should interrupt the innocent pleasure she was enjoying in his company, as he had frequently testified to them before by desiring them not to wake her. He says, therefore, Why do you so earnestly beseech my Bride to return that you may behold her? *What will you see in her* now that she is one with me, except *as it were the companies of an army in camp?* She has the grace and beauty of a company of young virgins, for the chaste kiss which I have bestowed upon her has infinitely increased her purity. She has at the same time the strength and terror of an army, because she is associated with the Holy Trinity and is made partaker of the divine attributes, who are in arms to fight and destroy all the enemies of God in her behalf?

O Prince's daughter! O Child of God! exclaim the young maidens, thy steps are fair both within and without; those within are very beautiful, because she may continually advance in God without any cessation of her rest. It is the enchanting beauty of this advance that it is a true rest, which hinders in nothing her progress, and a veritable progress, which does not in the least interfere with her rest; on the contrary, the greater the rest the greater the progress, and the swifter the progress the more tranquil the rest. The steps without are also full of beauty; for she is well ordered, being conducted by the will of God and led in the order of His providence. *How beautiful are thy feet with shoes!* every step being taken in the will of God, from which they never depart. *The joints of the thighs* indicate the admirable order of her actions, which take place with an entire subordination of the inferior to the superior part and of the superior to God. He is the *cunning workman* who has *melted* and shaped this soul in the furnace of Love.

Verse 2. Thy navel is like a round goblet which wanteth not liquor; thy belly is like a heap of wheat set about with lilies.

By the *navel* is intended the capacity of the soul to receive or the passive disposition which is extended and increased to an infinite degree, since she has been received into God; not solely for her own reception of divine communications, but also that she may conceive and bring forth many children to Jesus Christ. It is round, because it receives much but can contain nothing, receiving only to disperse. It is at the same time both fitted to receive and prompt in distributing, herein partaking of the qualities of the Bridegroom. It is continually full of liquor derived from the fountain head of Divinity, and the choicest graces are bestowed upon her for the benefit of others. Her *belly is like a heap of wheat;* for as that sprouts, grows, bears fruit and feeds the hungry, so her spiritual fecundity is abundant in similar excellencies. It is surrounded with lilies as a mark of the absolute purity of the whole.

Verse 3. Thy two breasts are like two young roes that are twins.

It would be a small matter for the Spouse to bear children to the Bridegroom, if he gave her nothing for their nourishment; the Bridegroom therefore here speaks of her breasts, to show that she is not only a mother, but a nurse. In truth, not only has she abundant nourishment for her children, but her breasts are always full, though they are incessantly emptied, and there is not an instant when some one is not making some demand upon them. Though they are thus constantly drawn they do not decrease, but on the contrary, their fulness increases with the graces they furnish, so that the measure of their supply is the measure of their fulness. They are very justly compared to the young twin roes, that we may understand that she derives what she dispenses wholly from God; for as the young roes depend upon their mother's breast, so the Spouse is always attached to Him from whom she receives whatever she communicates to others.

Verse 4. Thy neck is as a tower of ivory; thine eyes like the fish-pools in Heshbon, which are in the gate of the daughter of the multitude; thy nose is as the tower of Lebanon, which looketh toward Damascus.

The *neck* signifies strength; it is of *ivory,* because the purity of strength consists in being in God, and for this reason the strength of the Spouse is absolutely pure. Her strength is a *tower* where the soul is sheltered from every danger, and whence she discovers the approach of her enemies. The understanding is referred to as the *eyes,* and when this faculty is lost in God it is become a *fish-pool,* a source of every blessing and a remedy for every ill. God employs the mind which has been willingly given up for His sake, in a thousand great under-takings that are useful for the good of the neighbor. These pools are *at the gate of the daughters of the multitude.* This child of the multitude is no other than the imagination and fancy, which disturb and injure the clearness of the mind before the mystical division is effected. But now this is no longer the case, for she is no longer inconvenienced by the frivolous and impertinent intrusion of the senses; God having, as it were, set up a door between the spirit and the senses. The *nose* is the symbol of prudence, which is become *like the tower of Lebanon,* because it is strong and impregnable, being the very providence and prudence of God, bestowed upon the soul in consideration of its simplicity, by which it has lost all human prudence. This celestial prudence looks but one way: it sees nothing but the divine movement of Providence, and all its foresight consists in receiving what comes from moment to moment. O Prudence destitute of prudence! how dost thou surpass the prudence of men, even the most prudent!

Verse 5. Thine head upon thee is like Carmel, and the hair of thy head like the King's purple, bound by the water courses.

The *superior* part is like a mountain elevated into its God; and *the hair,* which represents all the gifts with which she has been favored, belongs so entirely to God that the Spouse has no longer any claim upon it. If she has any good or any possession, all belongs to Him; they are the property of the Bridegroom, so that all the adornments and embellishments of the superior part are *the royal purple,* since it is a partaking of the same ornaments wherewith the King is arrayed. But this purple is yet *attached to the water courses,* both to perfect the brilliancy of its color by the graces which descend from Heaven for it, and because it is in the soul as in a channel of distribution, which receives without resistance all the graces of her God, but suffers them all at the same time to run back into Him, without retaining any for herself; or rather, which only serves as a canal to give free passage to the rivers of grace that they may flow down to water the spiritual gardens.

Verse 6. How fair and how pleasant art thou, O Love, for delights!

God beholding in His Spouse His own perfections (reflected as in a faithful mirror), is enchanted with His own beauty contemplated in her, and exclaims, *How fair and how pleasant art thou* in My beauty, and how glorious is My beauty in thee! Thou art all My delight as I am the delight of My Father. For, representing Me to the life, as in a costly mirror, which produces no distortion in the objects held before it, thou givest Me an infinite pleasure. Thou art fair and enchanting, for thou art clothed with all My perfections. But if thou art My delight, I am also thine, and our pleasures are common to both.

Verse 7. This thy stature is like to a palmtree, and thy breasts to clusters of grapes.

Thy stature, that is, thy whole soul, is like to a palmtree, by reason of its uprightness. The favors with which I have loaded thee have not bent thee toward thyself; on the contrary, like a beautiful palm, thou art never more erect than when most heavily laden. The female palmtree has two peculiarities; one, that it is more upright the more fruit it bears, and the other that it will not bear at all except under the shadow of the male. In the same way this lovely soul has two peculiarities; one, that she never inclines in the least towards herself for any grace that she may have received of God; the other, that she cannot perform the slightest action, however insignificant, of herself, but does all things under the shadow of the Bridegroom who causes her to do everything in its season. *Her breasts* are beautifully likened *to clusters of grapes.* As the grape, though full of juice, receives none of it for herself, but yields it all to him that presses it; so this soul, the more she is oppressed and persecuted, becomes more and more benevolent and bountiful to those that evil entreat her.

Verse 8. I said, I will go up to the palmtree, and I will take hold of the fruit thereof; and thy breasts shall be as clusters of the vine, and the smell of thy mouth like that of apples.

The young virgins having heard the comparison made by the King of Glory, and transported with a desire to partake of the graces of the Spouse, cry out with one voice, or rather, one, expressing the feelings of the rest, exclaims, *I will go up to the palmtree, I will take hold of the fruits thereof;* I will become a pupil of this mistress of perfection, and if one so wise and so rich will condescend to become a mother to me, I will be her daughter, that I may experience the effects of the anointing of the Bridegroom, which is in her. The fruit of her words will be to me like a cluster of grapes of an exquisite sweetness, and the purity of her teaching will embalm me in its perfume.

Verse 9. Thy throat is like the best wine, fit for my beloved to drink, and to be dwelt upon with delight by his lips and teeth.

The young daughter of Zion continues in praise of the Spouse; by *her throat* she intends the interior of the soul, which is the best wine, for it is perfectly fluid and runs into God with out being hindered by any obstacle in its own consistence. It is a wine for God's drinking, for He receives the soul into Himself, changing and transforming her into Him; He makes her His pleasure and delight. He forms and reforms her, causing her more and more to disappear and to be more and more wonderfully transformed in Him. It is truly worthy to be the beverage of God, for she alone is capable of making it, and it is also worthy of the soul, since that is its sovereign good and final end.

Verse 10. I am my beloved's, and His desire is towards me.

The Spouse, being assured of the truth of the assertions of the virgins, confesses and even confirms it. Ever since the ardent love of my Well-beloved has wholly devoured me, I have been so lost in Him that I can no longer find myself, and I can say, with a more interior truth than ever before, that *I am my Beloved's,* since He has changed me into Himself; so that as He cannot any longer cast me off, I no longer fear any separation from Him.

O Love! Thou wilt no more repulse such a soul as this! and it may be said that she is confirmed in love forevermore, since she has been perfected by the same love and changed into Him. *The Well-beloved* now beholding nothing in His Spouse which is not absolutely of and for Him, can neither turn away His desire nor His looks from her, as He can never cease to behold and love Himself.

Verse 11. Come, my beloved, let us go forth into the field; let us lodge in the villages.

The Spouse can no longer fear anything, since everything has become God for her, and she finds Him equally in all things. She has no longer anything to do with means nor with being shut up and guarded; she has entered into a glorious participation of the immensity of God. Everything that is said of this ineffable union is understood, with all the essential differences between the Creator and the creature, though with a perfect unity of love and of mystical reflux into God alone. She no longer fears losing Him, since she is not only united to Him, but transformed into Him. Hence it is that she invites Him to go forth from the enclosure of the house or of the garden. *Come, my love,* she says, *let us* go over the world to conquer for Thee; there is now no place either too small or too large for me, since my place is God himself, and wherever I am, I am in my God.

Verse 12. Let us get up early to the vineyards; let us see if the vine flourish, if the flowers bring forth fruit, and the pomegranate has blossomed; there will I give thee my breasts.

She invites her Bridegroom to go everywhere, for she is now full of activity. And, as God is forever acting without and constantly at rest within, so this soul, confirmed within in perfect rest, is also exceedingly active without. What she did awhile ago defectively, she now does in perfection. It is no longer herself nor her fruits which she contemplates, but she sees everything in God. In the field of the church she beholds a thousand things to be done for the glory of the Bridegroom, and at these she labors with all her strength, according to the occasions presented by Providence, and in the whole extent of her calling.

But explain thyself, O lovely Spouse; what meanest thou by *giving thy breasts* to thy Bridegroom? Is it not He that renders them fruitful and fills them with milk? Ah! she means that being in perfect liberty of spirit and enlargedness of soul, since she has no longer any selfish mixture in laboring for His glory, she will give Him the whole fruit of her breasts, and will cause Him to drink the milk with which He fills them. He is their beginning and also their end, into which she desires that they shall be emptied.

Verse 13. The mandrakes give a smell, and at our gates are all manner of pleasant fruits, new and old, which I have laid up for thee, O my Beloved.

Admirable oneness! All things are common between the Bridegroom and the Spouse. As she has nothing that belongs to herself, the possessions of the Bridegroom become common to her also. She has no longer any property or any interests but His, and hence she says that young and advancing souls, *the mandrakes, give a smell;* it has reached even to us. All that I have, my Well-beloved, she says, is Thine, and all Thine is mine. I am so stripped and spoiled of all things, that I have preserved, given, and *laid up for Thee all manner of pleasant fruits,* all sorts of excellent actions and productions, whatsoever they may be, without a single exception. I have given Thee all my works, both the *old* which Thou didst perform in me from the beginning, and the *new* which Thou effectest by me from moment to moment. There is nothing which I have not surrendered to Thee; my soul, with all its powers and operations; my body, with its senses and everything that it can do. I have consecrated the whole to Thee, and as Thou hast given them to me to keep, permitting me the use, I preserve them wholly for Thee, so that both as to the property and the use, all things are Thine only.

CHAPTER 8

VERSE 1. Who will give thee to me for a brother, sucking the breasts of my mother! that I might find thee without and kiss thee, and yet not be despised?

THE Spouse demands a further sinking into deeper union. Though the transformed soul is in a permanent and enduring union, she is nevertheless like a spouse engaged about the concerns of the household, who must go hither and thither, though she does not cease to be the spouse. But beyond this, there are moments when the heavenly Bridegroom is pleased to embrace and caress His Bride more closely. This is what she now demands. *Who will give me,* she cries, *My Spouse, who is also my brother, for we sucked the breasts of my mother,* that is, the Divine Essence? Since He has hidden me with Himself in God, I draw with Him without ceasing at the breasts of Divinity. But, in addition to this inconceivable advantage, I would find Him alone *without,* that I might enjoy his tender caresses whereby I am more deeply sunk in Him. She also asks another grace

which is not granted until late; that the outward may
be changed and transformed like the inward; for the
interior is changed a long time in advance of the
exterior, so that for a considerable time certain slight
weaknesses remain, which serve to conceal the
abundance of grace, and do not displease the
Bridegroom. They are, nevertheless, a sort of
weakness that excites the contempt of the creature.
Let Him so transform my exterior then, cries the
Spouse, *that I shall not be despised!* What I ask is for
the glory of God, and not for my own gain, for I am
not able to regard myself any longer.

Verse 2. I will lay hold upon thee and bring thee into my mother's
house; there thou shalt teach me, and I will give thee a bowl of
spiced wine, and new wine of my pomegranates.

The soul finding herself thus intimately
connected with God, experiences two things. One is,
that her Bridegroom is in her as she is in Him, just as
an empty vase thrown into the ocean is full of the
same water by which it is surrounded, and contains
without comprehending that within which it is
contained, so that the soul who is borne by her
Bridegroom bears Him also. And whither does she
bear Him? thither only where she can go: she bears
Him *into the bosom of her* Father, which is her
mother's house, that is the place of her birth. The
other thing which she experiences is, that there He
instructs her, bestowing upon her the knowledge of
His secret things, which is only given to the favorite
Spouse, to whom He teaches every truth that is
necessary for her to know, or with which, from the
excess of His love, He desires that she should be
acquainted. O wonderful knowledge! communicated
with but little stir, in the ineffable but ever eloquent

silence of the Divinity. The Word unceasingly speaks to the soul, and instructs her in such way as to shame the most enlightened teachers.

But in proportion as He teaches the soul, insinuating Himself by degrees more and more into her, and continually enlarging her passive capacity, the faithful soul *causes Him to drink of her spiced wine and of the new wine of her pomegranates.* This is the fruit of charity in her, for she perpetually offers up to Him everything which He confers upon her, in the greatest purity. There is a constant flux and reflux of intercommunications; the Bridegroom bestowing upon the Bride and the Bride rendering to the Bridegroom. O incomparable Spouse! shall I say it? Thou art partaker of the intercourse of the Holy Trinity, for thou receivest without ceasing and renderest as incessantly what thou receivest.

Vesre 3. His left hand should be under my head, and his right hand should embrace me.

As we have before said, God has two arms with which He holds and embraces the Spouse; *one* is His omnipotent protection, by which He supports her; *the other* is the perfect love with which He embraces her, and this holy embrace is no other than the enjoyment of Himself and essential union. When the Spouse here declares that His hand should embrace her, she is not speaking of something that has not taken place, but is yet to come to pass, since she received this divine embrace with the nuptial kiss; but she speaks of it as always present and always to come, since it shall be continued throughout eternity.

The Bridegroom charges three separate times
that His love be not awaked from her sleep, because
there are three different sorts of interior slumber.
The first is in the union of the powers, in which she
enjoys a sleep of a powerful ecstasy, which extends
much over the senses. He then begs that she may not
be awakened, because this sleep is then of use to
detach the senses from the objects which they loved
impurely, and thus to purify them.

The second is the sleep of mystical death, where
she expires in the arms of love. Neither is He willing
she should be disturbed in this, until she awakes of
herself by the all-powerful voice of God, summoning
her from the tomb of death to the spiritual
resurrection.

The third is the slumber of repose in God,
permanent, lasting; an ecstatic rest, but sweet, calm
and enduring, occasioning no alteration in the senses,
the soul having passed into God by her happy
deliverance from self. This is a rest from which she
shall never be disturbed. He would not that His
beloved should be interfered with in any of their
slumbers, but that they should be permitted to be at
rest, for they sleep in His arms.

The first repose is a promised rest, of which
pledges are given; the second is a rest bestowed, and
the third is a rest confirmed, whereof there shall be
no further interruption. Not that it could not be
broken, for she is still at liberty, and the Bridegroom
would not say *until she please,* if she had no longer

the power to will it; but after a union of this kind, except we suppose the extremist ingratitude and infidelity, she would never do so.

In the meanwhile the Divine Bridegroom, while He eulogizes His Spouse and permits others to praise her in his presence, desires at the same time continually to instruct her. In order to show her that nothing but a vain self-complacency and contempt of others can give rise to so deplorable a result as a departure from Him, He, in the next verse, sets before her the baseness of her origin and the vileness of her nature, so that she may never lose sight of her humility.

Verse 5. Who is this that cometh up from the wilderness, replete with delights, leaning upon the arm of her beloved? I raised thee up under the appletree; there thy mother was corrupted, there was she deflowered that brought thee forth.

The soul has come up gradually from the desert since she abandoned it; not only the desert of pure faith, but of self. She runs over with delights because she is full, and like a vessel filled to the brim with water from the spring, runs over on all sides for the supply of those about her. She is no longer self-supported, and hence she no longer fears the abundance of these delights. She does not fear being overthrown, for her Well-beloved, who sheds them into her bosom, carries them Himself with her, and suffers her to walk, leaning upon Him.

O precious gain, the loss of all created stays! God Himself is received for our sole support, in exchange for them!

I raised thee up under the appletree. I drew thee from the sleep of mystical death, raising thee from self, from thine own corruption and from the spoiled and corrupted nature which thy mother gave thee by her sin. For all the operations of God in the soul tend towards two things: one, to deliver it from its actual wickedness and the malignity of its depraved nature, the other, to restore it to God as fair and as pure as it was before Eve fell under the power of the seducer. In her innocence, Eve belonged to God without any self-appropriation; but she suffered herself to be violated, withdrawing herself from God to commit prostitution with the Devil, and we have all partaken of the evil consequences of that act. We come into the world like illegitimate children, who have no idea of their real Father, and who cannot be recognized as belonging to God until they are legitimated by baptism. But even then they have still the traces of that wretched sin; they retain a malign quality opposed to God, until He, by long, powerful and repeated operations removes it, drawing the soul out of self, depriving it of all its infection, re-endowing it with the grace of innocence, and causing it to be lost in Him. He thus *raises it from under the appletree,* and innocent being, from the very place where its mother, human nature, had been corrupted.

Verse 6. Set me as a seal upon thy heart, as a seal upon thine arm; for love is strong as death, jealousy is cruel as hell; the lights thereof are lights of fire and flames.

The Bridegroom invites the Spouse to *set Him as a seal upon her heart;* for as He is the source of her life, He ought also to be its seal. It is He who hinders her from ever leaving so blessed a state; she is then the fountain sealed, which none but Himself can either open or shut. He desires also that she should set Him *as a seal* upon her exterior and her works, so that everything may be reserved for Him and nothing may move without His directions. She is then a garden enclosed for her Bridegroom, which He shuts and no man opens, and opens and no man shuts. *For love,* says the Bridegroom, *is as strong as death,* to do what he pleases in His beloved. He is strong as death, inasmuch as He causes her to die to everything that she may live to Him only. *But jealousy is cruel as hell,* and therefore He encloses His Spouse so carefully. So strong is His desire for her utter devotion to Himself, that if we conceive her guilty of the infidelity of withdrawing her abandonment, a supposition as melancholy as it is difficult, she would be instantaneously repulsed from Him into hell by the excess of His indignation. The lamps are lamps of fire which enlighten while they burn, and consume while giving light.—O Lamb, who openest and shuttest the seven seals! So seal up Thy Beloved that she may no more go forth except by and for Thee; for she is Thine by an everlasting marriage.

Verse 7. Many waters cannot quench love, neither can the floods drown it; if a man would give all the substance of his house for love, it would utterly be contemned.

If the manifold waters of afflictions, contradictions, miseries, poverty and distresses have not been able to quench the love of this soul, it is not to be supposed that the floods of abandonment to the Divine Providence could do it, for it is they that preserve it. If a man has had courage enough to abandon all the substances of his house and himself also that he may possess this pure love, which can only be acquired by the loss of all the rest, it is not to be believed that, after so generous an effort to acquire a good which he values above all other things, and which in truth is worth more than the whole universe, he will afterwards so underrate it as to return to what he had abandoned. It is not possible; God by this shows us the assuredness and persistence of this state, and how difficult it is for a soul who has reached it, ever to leave it again.

Verse 8. We have a little sister and she hath no breasts; what shall we do for our sister in the day when she shall be spoken for?

The Spouse is so happy with her Bridegroom that they have all things in common between them. She speaks with Him of the affairs of other souls, and converses familiarly with Him as though of their household matters. *What shall we do,* she says, for this soul, still *little* and tender, who is *our sister* by reason of her purity and simplicity; (she refers to all like her in the person of one). *What shall be done for her in the day when I must begin to communicate with her? For as yet she hath no breasts,* nor sufficient inclination for the divine marriage; she is not in a condition to assist others; how shall we do with her? This is the way in which the Spouse should consult with Jesus on behalf of souls.

Verse 9. If she be a wall, we will build upon it bulwarks of silver; if she be a door we will frame it with boards of cedar.

The Bridegroom replies: if she be already *a wall* of confidence through a well established passivity, we will begin *to build upon her bulwarks of silver,* for her defence against the enemies of this advanced state, which are human reason, reflection and the subtlety of self-love. But, *if she is as yet but a door,* just beginning to emerge from multiplicity to enter into simplicity, we will frame her with graces and virtues which shall have the beauty and solidity of *cedar.*

Verse 10. I am a wall, and my breasts like towers; then was I in his eyes as one that found favor.

The Spouse, in ecstasies at the instruction and promise which she has just received from the mouth of the Bridegroom, instances herself as an example of the success of this plan. *I am* myself, she cries, *a wall of such strength and my breasts are like a tower,* which may serve as an asylum and defence to a multitude of souls and which keeps me also in assurance, since *I was in His eyes as one that had found peace* in God that shall never be lost.

Verse 11. The Peaceable One hath a vineyard, which hath people in it; he delivered it to keepers, each one brings for the fruit thereof a thousand pieces of silver.

It seems, O my God, as though Thou hadst taken pleasure in forestalling all the doubts and objections that could possibly arise. It might be supposed that this soul, no longer possessing herself and no more performing any works, no longer had any merit. Thou, O God, art this God of Peace, that has a vineyard whereof the principal care is entrusted to Thy Spouse, and the Spouse herself is the vineyard. She is placed in a spot which is called *people;* for Thou hast rendered Thy Spouse fruitful and mother of an innumerable people. Thou hast commissioned Thine angels as the keepers, and it brings in a great profit both to Thee, O God, and to the soul herself.

Thou givest her the privilege of using and partaking of the fruits; she has the advantage of being scarcely any longer in danger of losing or of displeasing Thee, and, at the same time, of not ceasing to profit and to merit ever.

Verse 12. My vineyard is before me; Thou, O Peaceable, must have a thousand, and those that keep the fruit thereof, two hundred.

The chaste Spouse no longer declares as she formerly did: *I have not kept my vineyard.* It was then a vineyard, the charge of which men desired to impose upon her contrary to the will of God; but, as to this one, committed to her as it is by her Bridegroom, ah! what care does she not expend upon it! All things which are in the order of God, agree perfectly well with all kinds of employments, whether interior or exterior, and everything is done with wonderful facility, as soon as the person who is charged with it is brought into perfect liberty. The faithfulness of the Spouse is worthy of all admiration: for, though she watches with so much care the cultivation and care of the vineyard, she nevertheless leaves the whole revenue to the Bridegroom, giving the keepers an equitable salary, but retaining nothing for herself. Perfect love does not know what it is to consider self-interest.

Verse 13. Thou that dwellest in the gardens, the companions hearken to thy voice; cause me to hear it.

The Bridegroom invites his Spouse to speak in his behalf, and to enter actually upon the Apostolic life by teaching others. *Thou, O my Spouse,* He says, *that dwellest in the gardens,* in the ever-flowered parterres of the Divinity, where thou hast not ceased to dwell since the winter has passed, thou hast been in gardens as beautiful for the variety of the flowers with which it was adorned as for the excellence of the fruits which abound there; thou, O My Spouse, whom I keep constantly with Me in these gardens of delights, leave, for a moment, the rest full of sweetness and silence which thou there enjoyest, *and cause Me to hear thy voice, for thy companions hearken.*

In these words the Bridegroom requires of His Spouse two things equally admirable. One, that she may depart from the profound silence in which she has hitherto remained. During the whole time of faith and her loss in God, she remained in great silence, because it was necessary to reduce her entire being into the simplicity and unity of God alone; now that she is entirely confirmed in this oneness, He desires to bestow upon her, as a fruit of her completed state, the admirable harmony of multiplicity and unity, wherein the multiplicity does not interfere with the unity nor the unity with the multiplicity. He desires that she should add to the silent word of the centre, which is the state of unity, the outward praise of the mouth. This is a faint image of what will take place in glory, where, after the soul has been absorbed for ages in an ineffable silence ever eloquent of the Divinity, she will receive her glorified body, which will give sensible praise to the Lord. Thus, after the resurrection, the body will have its own language of praise, which will add to the happiness and not diminish the peace of the soul.

In this life even, when the soul is perfected in a oneness which can no more be interrupted by external actions, the mouth of the body is endued with a praise appropriate to it, and the beautiful harmony between the silent word of the soul and the sensible speech of the body constitutes the perfection of praise. The soul and the body render praise conformable to what they are; the praise of the mouth alone is not praise; thus God says by the Prophet, *This people honoreth me with their lips but have removed their heart far from me*. The praise which comes purely from the depths of the soul, being dumb, and so much the more so as it is more perfect, is not an absolutely complete adoration; for man being composed of soul and body, both should join in giving praise. The perfection of adoration then, is, that the body shall give forth its praise of such sort that far from interrupting the deep and ever eloquent silence of the centre of the soul, it rather increases it, and that the silence of the soul shall be no hindrance to the utterance of the body, which knows how to render appropriate worship to its God. Thus perfect adoration, both in time and eternity, has reference to this resurrection of the exterior word in unity with the interior.

But the soul, accustomed to deep and ineffable silence, is fearful of interrupting it, and thus has some difficulty in resuming the exterior word. Wherefore the Bridegroom, to rid her of this imperfection, is obliged to invite her to let her voice be heard. *Cause me to hear thy voice,* He exclaims. It is time to speak; to speak to Me with thy bodily voice, that thou mayest praise Me as thou hast learned to do during thy admirable silence. There is besides an interior and wholly unspeakable word, God endowing the soul with liberty of conversing with Him at times according to His good pleasure, with great facility. He invites her also to talk to souls about interior things, and to teach them what to do that they may be agreeable to Him. It is one of the principal functions of the Spouse, to instruct and teach the interior life to the beloved of the Bridegroom, who have not as near access to Him as the Shulamite.

This, then, is what the Bridegroom desires of the Spouse; that she address Him both with heart and voice, and that she speak to others for Him.

Verse 14. Flee away, my beloved, and be thou like to a roe or to a young hart upon the mountains of spices.

The soul having now no other interest than that of the Bridegroom, either for self or for any other creature, and who can will nothing except His glory, seeing something which dishonors Him, cries out, *Flee away, my Beloved!* Leave these places which offer Thee no perfume. Come to those souls who are as *mountains of spices,* raised above the fetid vapors corrupted by the wickedness of this world. These mountains owe their sweetness to the odor of the exquisite virtues which Thou hast planted in them, and it is only in such souls that Thou wilt find true repose.

The soul, arrived at this point, enters so fully into the interests of the Divine Righteousness, both in respect to herself and others, that she can desire no other fate for herself, nor for any other, than that which the Divine Righteousness would allot, both for time and eternity. She has at the same time a more

perfect charity than ever before for the neighbor,
serving him now for God only, and in the will of God.
But though she is always ready to be cursed for her
brethren, like St. Paul, and is incessantly laboring for
no other end than their salvation, she is nevertheless
indifferent as to her success. She would not be
afflicted either at her own damnation or at that of any
other creature, regarded from the point of view of
God's Righteousness. What she cannot bear is, that
God should be dishonored, because He has set love in
order within her; since then she has entered into the
purest affections of perfect charity.

We must not suppose that the soul in the state of
this Spouse is constantly eager for the sensible
presence and sweet and continual enjoyment of the
Bridegroom. By no means. She was once in that state
of perfection in which she ardently longed for that
delightful possession; it was necessary *then* to attract
her on in her progress towards Him; but now it
would be an imperfection which she must not
entertain; her Well-beloved, in truth, possessing her
perfectly in her essence and powers, in a very real
and unchangeable manner, above all time and place
and means. She has no more to do with sighing for
seasons of distinct and conscious enjoyment; and,
besides, she is in such an absolute state of
abandonment as to everything, that she could not
fasten a desire of any kind upon anything whatever,
not even upon the delights of Paradise. And this state
is even the evidence that she is possessed at the
centre. This is why she here testifies to the
Bridegroom that she is satisfied He should go where
He pleases, visit other hearts, gain them, purify them,
and perfect them in all the mountains and hills of the
church; that He should take His delight in *souls of*

spices, embalmed in grace and virtue; but, for herself, she has nothing to ask or desire of Him except He himself be the author of the emotion. Does she therefore despise or reject the divine visits and consolators? not at all; she has too much respect and submission for the work of God to do that; but such graces are no longer adapted to her state, annihilated as she is, and established in the enjoyment of the centre; having lost all her will in the will of God, she can no longer will anything. This is beautifully expressed in the verse cited.

So great is the indifference of this soul, that she cannot lean either to the side of enjoyment or deprivation. Death and life are equally acceptable; and although her love is incomparably stronger than it ever was before, she cannot, nevertheless, desire Paradise, because she remains in the hands of her Bridegroom, as among the things that are not. Such is the effect of the deepest annihilation.

Although she is in this state more than ever fitted for the help of souls, and serves with extreme care those sent to her by the Bridegroom, she cannot have a desire to assist others, nor can she even do it without the special direction of Providence.

Made in the USA
Coppell, TX
09 April 2020